Introduction

Hello. Let me introduce myself. My name is Victor Avon, and I have an eating disorder. Now that I have your attention, I feel like we can get down to business. I know what you are saying: "But wait Vic, you are a man, and men do not get eating disorders". The vast majority of people out there know very little about the subject of eating disorders. If I had to guess, I would say that when most people think of a person with an eating disorder they think of a ~~ ~~ ~~ heir teenage years that wa~~ ee that just about everyor~~ be a female. Well, unfortu~~ ~~~ ~~uth is that men can, and do, get eating disorders. I was caught within the throws of an eating disorder that was so bad at points that I was told by professionals within the field that my case was the worst that they have ever seen or heard of. It was the force that drove me, the weight that held me down, the hole I hid in, but most importantly, it was the monster I had within.

Currently, I am 26 years old and have lived within the dark world of an eating disorder for the past seven years. In those seven years, I experienced a wide range of emotions and have risen to greats highs and crashed down to severe lows. I thought the eating disorder was giving me freedom and life, while actually it took my freedom and my life from me. I made a "friend" that I kept a secret from everyone, hid from everyone, protected from everyone, and almost died as a result of. Through many trials and tribulations of my own, and ultimately the help of intense therapy and hospitalization I was finally able to loosen the grip my "friend" had on me and walk on the path to recovery, which is where I stand today.

I started writing the book you are about to read in late 2006 just after I began my first round of treatment, in hopes of changing my life around. The therapist I was seeing at the time did not teach me any coping skills to help with what I was going through, so one day I just sat down and started typing. I started writing this to try to make some sense of my whole situation. I knew I had some kind of problem, but was lost in the dark about everything. I was confused about what was happening to me, confused about why I felt the way I did, confused about why I did things in certain ways, and confused about why it all began. In essence I just started typing to find out the what, why, and how of my circumstances. Words just flowed from my fingers, from the second I began typing. It seemed as if I had tapped into something I had never used, thought about, or expressed before. Overall, however, I had no intentions to do anything with this project, and never planned to add anything else after I was finished with the initial 30 pages, but for some reason I kept revisiting it and adding more and more at different points in time. It became more than a project. It was something personal. It was a way for me to vent. It was my journal, and it was going to be my record if and when something ever happened to me.

The piece of literature before you was written at several different points in time, much like a diary, and is broken down just as I had originally typed it. There are gaps ranging from a few months to a year between each section, starting from the beginning of my treatment and concluding with where I am today. I have not done much editing because I wanted you to be able to understand where I was emotionally during each period.

I realized very early in my hospitalization, after the suggestion by my doctor and therapist, that I would like to publish and share my story with others. After much soul searching I realized that maybe I could help others by showing them what I went through. I thought that I may be able to help a parent or family member have a little more understanding of the disease, or maybe help someone who is currently suffering with their own disorder. By relating to what I went through, they will know that they are not suffering alone out there. A big reason why I want my story to get out there is because I feel there needs to be more of an understanding that eating disorders affect a significant number of men. The stigma that this is a "girl's disease" causes many men not to "come out" and get treatment. There are hundreds of books that cover the subject of eating disorders. I have come upon only two books so far that deal with men and eating disorders, both of which were not that good in my opinion (and one ultimately worsened my condition as you will see later). The majority of resources, whether they are websites, informational literature, or treatments programs/facilities, are geared to help women. The majority of men that suffer with these disorders are forced to suffer in silence due to the intense feelings of shame and embarrassment. I hope that I may help ease their suffering. If this book helps one single person then I will have accomplished everything that I have set out to do. With that said, I invite you to read "my story" and learn about my monster within.

Part 1

Have you ever wondered what it feels like to have no control over yourself? Have you ever wondered what it is like to have every thought and action being controlled by something else? Most importantly, have you ever wondered what it is like to lose the desire to live? My life has been a constant struggle. Since the early part of 2002, a war has been waging inside of me. My mind and my body have turned against me, to the point where I feel like a broken man. This book attempts to put in writing all of the experiences in my short life that may have caused me to turn out the way that I have. As you read this I want you to remember one thing: Living like this is not a choice, I wouldn't choose to live like this. This is my story.

My earliest memories when I can truly remember my feelings toward life are from my years living at 442 Park Ave in Fairview, New Jersey. I may have been very young, but I remember not having contempt for life. I had good, stable friendships with

Harut and Seto, the two Armenian brothers that lived around the corner, and was living life like an average kid. My family struggled financially and lived from paycheck to paycheck. I give my parents a lot of credit for being able to do what they did with three kids and little income. I was able to learn the value of a buck, and what it takes to live using the change that was thrown in the big water jug. We were poor, but we were happy. I had no "wants" as a kid. I was taught to be respectful and polite, and that is how I acted. I never gave anybody any type of grief and would like to think that I was an "all around" good kid. I'm not trying to depict myself as an angelic/saintly little kid, but I do believe that I was a physically and emotionally healthy child. My grandparents lived about a mile away in Cliffside Park, and my family spent a considerable amount of time at their house. I have considered my grandparents to be the greatest people in my life and they may have had more of an influence on my early development than my parents did. We had very caring neighbors that lived on our immediate right on Park

Ave. Mayo and Mildred Cavari were an elderly couple with hearts of gold and welcomed my brother, my sister, and I into their home as if we were their own grandchildren.

Physically, I remember being a husky child. I was not fat, in the sense of what we think fat kids are, but was somewhat big. Being big was a result of a few elements of my life. First, my body structure is big. The men on my dad's side of the family are all very big men so I inherited their body type. I was also brought up in an Italian home, being constantly bombarded with macaroni and other foods that one would not consider "good" for himself or herself (the deep fried foods, sugary foods, etc.). I had to eat everything on my plate, a value that was pounded into me from my father. There was usually a second helping being plated for me when my first one was finished. My Nana and Pops loved to feed us. They took great pleasure in making sure everybody had enough to eat. My Nana worked in the high school cafeteria before I was born, always threw the big family dinners and barbeques, and spent

25 years cooking for the senior citizens of Cliffside Park. She basically got her rocks off by serving people and making them feel good with food. Also, my grandfather worked in the vending industry. It was only natural to him to try and make us happy by bringing home cases of all the chips and candy bars on the market (what he called "pickings") and cans upon cans of all the sodas imaginable. Nothing made my grandparents happier than filling my plate over and over again, and seeing that smile on my young face.

I have always been a bit quiet. I am not very outgoing and have never been comfortable around people that I do not know. I was always reserved and private (especially in my older years). I was usually a follower in a group. I would often submit and go along with what everybody else wanted to do. I can remember Harut and Seto being the ones that called the shots as to what we did and where we went, but I was never really bothered by this. It was just the way I naturally was. One thing that bothers me is that I have always been too afraid to stand up for myself or stand up for what I believed in when I should have. I would "chicken out" and submit and just hold what I was feeling inside of me. This would bother me because my father always filled my head with what he felt a "man" should do: "Stand up for yourself, beat him up if he did that to you, don't take any shit from anybody", etc. It was always an internal dilemma for me. I wasn't sure of myself. I always seemed to have inner turmoil in my life, one way or another.

Life changed a little bit around the age of 10. I switched schools from Public School Number Three in Fairview to the Epiphany School in Cliffside Park. Epiphany was a Catholic school with small class sizes and schooled kids from kindergarten to the eighth grade. I knew I was going to be attending a new school, but I did not know how hard it would be. I remember starting my first day of fifth grade and how awkward it was sitting in a room of kids that all knew each other. The class had about thirty students in it. They had all been going to school together for the past few years and now I was taken away from the friends that I knew and thrown into this new environment. I do remember being optimistic about my situation on the first day of school because my mother took my siblings and I to McDonalds after school and three of the girls in my class were so excited that the "cute" new kid was there. It made me happy; however, it was not going to be like this for very long. The adjustment was hard. I didn't make friends easily because of my not-so-outgoing personality. I kept to myself. The schoolwork was not easy for me. To make things more difficult Epiphany taught Spanish to students starting in the fifth grade, and I remember having an extremely hard time with the language. I would study and study and study with my mother and would still manage to fail tests.

The problems with my work and my attempts to socially fit in caused me much stress and emotional discomfort. It seemed like the only thing that made me feel better was the food that surrounded me. I ate almost everything that was in front of me. I ate all of the food that my mother and grandparents cooked, all the "pickings" that my grandfather brought home and shoved in my face, all the Vinny's pizza and McDonalds I could get my little hands on, etc. I remember gaining a lot of weight during that year. I went from the husky kid to the official "fat kid" of the class. As a result, not many people wanted to be friends with the "fat kid", and those three girls at the McDonalds no longer thought of me as the "cute" kid.

I was never self-conscious about my body before this time, but two incidents changed all of this. First, the boys of the class were being checked for scoliosis and were in the library waiting our turns to have our spines examined. I unbuttoned and took off my uniform dress shirt and was standing there when one kid (Jeremy Winters) told me that the girls were being checked in the other room. He was talking about my breasts and I can still remember this moment perfectly clear to this day. As a defense mechanism I crossed my arms over my "boobs" and tried to hide the best I could. The second incident occurred when the boys from the 5th and 6th grades were told to go down to the basement of the school. When we got there we were told that we were going to have physicals. I did not know what a physical was and all I knew was that when they called my name I was to go behind a walled off area of the room. When it was my turn I got up and went behind the wall where I was told to take my shirt off. Then a few minutes later I was told to take my pants down and stand there in my underwear. I stood there and then I realized that an entire section of this wall was open. All the kids in my class could see me standing there, and they all had this look on their faces like they wanted to burst out laughing. I started panicking inside my head, but I kept my composure. Then the doctor told me that he had to check me out for a hernia. I did not know what he was doing as he reached into my underwear and grabbed my balls and told me to cough. I remember when it was all said and done and I was sent back to the classroom, I felt like I was going to throw up. I was traumatized and completely freaked out. Everybody saw me almost naked, laughed at me, and then this stranger grabbed my balls. I was devastated. This did little to help my already fragile self-esteem and submissive personality. It was the catalyst to my body image/self-consciousness problems.

Sixth, Seventh, and Eighth grades were better, but not ideal. I was able to make a few friends with a group of people and was able to sustain my relationship with Harut and Seto, although they often put me down when we were around other kids. That's the one thing about those two that really bothered me. They were the greatest people when it was just us, but as soon as other kids were around I seemed to be the whipping post to make them look cool. The kids in the older grades often made fun of me. I was an easy target, and they took advantage of it. I never stood up to them and was depressed because I did not have the balls to do what my dad and other members of my family had always told me to do. I was too afraid, too submissive, too timid, and too unsure of myself. My food and weight situation did not change much in these years. I would eat constantly while home or by Pops' house and would often eat when I was out, especially when out with my friends. Everything seemed to involve food. It was everywhere and I loved it. I remember feeling sorry for myself because I was fat and had all of these social problems, many because I was fat, but I did little or nothing at all to remedy it. I did not like being fat, but I turned to food to make me feel better, thus adding more fuel to the fire. It was a vicious cycle. Food made me feel good. It never made fun of me, but at the same time I hated what it did to me. Overall, though, I did have some good times at the Epiphany School and despite my situation I was as happy as I could be there.

It is important to talk about my family situation during these early years. I can easily say that three people raised me: my mother, Pops, and Nana. My mother was there for everything. Whether it was getting us up and driving to school, going on rainy Saturday movie outings where we snuck in 3 different movies and brought our own popcorn, little campouts in the living room, or going to the Ridgefield pool, my mom took us everywhere and did a lot for us. My two siblings and I grew very close to my mom as a result. I do not remember my father playing a significant part in my early life. My dad was trying to get his company started and trying to provide better futures for all of us, but as a result he was noticeably absent from the picture. He was always on the road. He would leave before we woke up in the morning and get home around 6-7 o'clock at night. Once home I can remember him wanting to rest and watch television in "his" seat on the couch. He was often stressed, constantly on the telephone, and not very personable from what I remember. He was there, but he was not "there". There would be weeks where he was not there at all. He would go on road trips, or leave so early and get home so late that we never saw him. On the other hand, there were Pops and Nana, who were there for everything, all the time. Pops played the paternal role in my life, and I consider the man the greatest person in my life. He was the father when my father was not there. He taught me how to play basketball, taught me how to hit a baseball, kick a football, and spent time watching television, movies, and WWF with me. He would take me to the Meadowlands to see the WWF wrestlers. He was everything to me while my dad really wasn't, and I never felt like he ever judged me. Nana was on an equal level. She was very loving and caring and always looking to make me happy. She is my second mother. To be fair, though, my dad did do a lot for me. He did take me to Giants games, to Bear Mountain, and other such things. He did what he could with very little time and money to do it with. Let me make one thing clear: I currently understand why he did this, and truly appreciate and respect him for it, but at the time I was too young to understand. One early memory that I will not forget is when my dad took me to Madison Square Garden to see Hulk Hogan fight Sgt. Slaughter for the WWF championship. He did much for me and I can see this now, I just wish I knew it then.

One thing that often bothered me about my dad was that when I had sports practice or a game, he either would not be there or would criticize the way I was performing (at least that is how I felt at the time). He was a great athlete when he was younger and I felt that I had to perform at his level. Pops, however, was there for every single practice and every single game. He was my support (even with a bag of pickings and a Coke for when I was done). Pops always said I did a great job even though, more often than not, I hadn't played that well. I often resented my dad for not being there, to the point where I did not consider him my father.

Upon graduating from Epiphany I entered Cliffside Park High School. I entered this school with a few members from my Epiphany graduating class as well as a group of my friends from Fairview. On my first day there I decided to play football again because of the mix of people that were joining the team. From the first day of practice I felt enormous performance pressure. Every male in my family has played football at Cliffside High School at one point or another. My father has a legacy in CPHS football. He is considered to be among the best players the school has every seen. Two of the coaches that I was playing under either played with my father or had coached my father. It was very hard because expectations were extremely high from them, and I felt pressure to keep up to their standards and make my dad proud. It was hard also because I was out of shape at the time, but I loved the experience the season gave me. The best thing about it was the feeling of camaraderie the team brought me. I felt like I belonged, a feeling I had not had in a long time. We never won a game that season, but I felt like I had proved myself as I went from the second team to starting on the kick receiving team and starting defensive end. Pops made his way to watch every single practice and every single game (away and home). My dad, on the other hand, never came to one practice and only came to one game, (mainly) because it was a home game. He never showed me the interest or attention that I wanted from him. He never saw me start a game, which still disappoints me to this day.

I loved Cliffside High School. I was actually comfortable with life, but this all came crashing down. My parents thought it would be the best thing for my brother, sister, and I to move down to Wall, NJ and get out of the urban area that Fairview had become. On December 4, 1996 I was taken away from what I was growing to love and placed in a situation I had never thought possible. Wall Township was totally different than Fairview/Cliffside. It was very rural and high-class with no real sense of community and no neighborhood corners to hang out on. My first day at Wall High was extremely uncomfortable. First off, I had to take a bus for the first time in my life. Second, I was surrounded by a few hundred kids that were nothing like the kids I was used to. They were all "surfers", "Dead Heads", "stoners", etc. They were all different and I knew absolutely nobody, but I did not expect the reaction I was going to receive over the next few months.

I went into Wall High expecting it to be similar to my experiences starting out Epiphany and Cliffside High, hard at first but everything would be all right in a short amount of time. My expectations turned out to be as far from reality as one can imagine. People, especially young people, can be extremely insensitive and evil when they want to. My first few weeks at Wall were uncomfortable, but that was to be expected and nothing much to cry about. Once the holidays ended, the whole school decided to turn on me and treat me like I was nothing more than a piece of shit. I was ostracized by everybody. Nobody wanted anything to do with me, and those that did only had words of hate and/or wanted to make fun of me. I was tormented because I was different. I dressed a little different, had a different haircut, had an accent when I talked, and was fat. I was teased and made to feel like I was worthless. I remember being called the "fat fuck". I remember being in gym class and hearing people openly saying from across the gym that I "would suck a dick for a dollar" (in front of a teacher that did nothing about it). I remember two girls grabbing my ass in the hall way and then laughing hysterically when I confronted them (I can still hear their laughs to this day). I remember it all. Even the people that I thought were starting to be friends with me still busted me at times. As a result I hated life and I hated everybody in it. I wanted friends. I wanted companionship. I wanted to get close to someone. But every time I tried I was met by hate and pain. For the rest of my freshman year, entire sophomore year, and at least half of my junior year, I hung out with absolutely nobody and did nothing with anybody outside of my family. This hurt my social skills, as they were not allowed to develop like a normal person. I was shy and unsure about how to communicate with people as it was, and the fact that I had no real interaction with people for those important years really messed me up to the point that it took me a very long time to be comfortable interacting with people. I was not wanted, at least that was how I felt. I had a developed a stutter when I was younger, which still lingers to this day. It got worse during these terrible times. The stutter first developed while in Epiphany school, and caused me many hardships and stress then. Over time I seemed to work my way through it and succeeded to a point where it was barely noticeable. I remember being extremely self-conscious about the stutter, and was always very paranoid about the possibility of it ever becoming a major part of my life again. I grew extremely anxious and ultimately internally panicked when it reared its ugly head. It quickly got worse during my high school years. A stutter is one of the most frustrating and debilitating things a person can have because it makes one even more unsure of him or herself. It makes that person dread having to speak even more than they already do. It is one of those things that if a person has never experienced it, then he or she cannot understand how debilitating it really is. I know that I personally hated speaking because not only did I have extreme difficulty getting the actual words out, but also it just gave people one more thing to make fun of me for. This in turn, causes the stutter to get worse. I often felt that teachers even enjoyed hearing my troubles speaking as they would repeatedly call on me to answer questions, read aloud, or speak in front of the class. It seemed like nobody gave a damn about how I felt and how much discomfort I was in. All they wanted was for me to talk. I was the freak in the freak show that they found amusement in. I just felt like I was still that fat kid standing in front of the class in my underwear getting the physical. It broke me down. It destroyed my self-esteem and my self-confidence. It made me feel worthless. It made me want to die.

Things were not easy at home either. I remember resenting my father and being very angry with him for a very long time. I refused to speak to him. I did not want to acknowledge him mainly because I was mad at him for not being there for me in the years prior. The other reason for not speaking to him or most other people was because I was ashamed of what was happening to me at school and the inner turmoil I was going through. My mother did realize that something was wrong and called the principal one day, but nothing was really done. It seemed like he and the one teacher that he had talked to did not care. They only did as much as they were supposed to (call the kids in and tell them to stop), but I can tell that they never wanted to help. There was never a follow-up, never a check-in, etc. They just gave the wolves more reasons to pick me apart. Wall HS was like that. They were not out to protect the weak "nobodies" of the school, they were only interested in the jocks and popular kids. The only time that principal cared about me was when he wanted to suspend me for writing something on a doctor's note. He claimed that I forged the note and made me feel like a piece of shit in his office. This one incident severely hurt me because I did nothing wrong and now the faculty of the school was treating me like a criminal and did not care about anything that I had to say. The one who was supposed to protect me was making me feel the same as all of the kids in the school did. As a result I broke down and cried right there in his office. Everybody really was against me.

During this period, I feel that a new Vic was created. I withdrew into myself even further and created a new personality and view of life as a defense mechanism. For the next two to three years I really did not speak to anybody. I spent my lunch periods sitting by myself, and when I was home I spent most of my time in my room alone. I did not trust anybody. I would not let anybody get close to me at all. In the beginning I would cry, but eventually bottled up my emotions to the point that I became emotionless. I did not show my emotions at all. I did not show love. I did not show sorrow. I did not show much of anything. Showing my emotions led to pain in the past and the best way for me to get through everything was to learn not to show them at all, no matter how much I was hurting inside. I built a wall around me and hid behind it for years. My parents knew little about my situation because I did not want them to know. The only one that knew was me and I wanted everything that was happening to end, even if it meant ending my life. I sat in my room contemplating suicide on more than one occasion, but never took any overt action to get it done. I was even too chicken to kill myself. I would sit there wondering "Is life worth living? How could my life get to this point? What is wrong with me? Why did people do this to me? Am I so bad?"

There is an old phrase that most people know: "If you tell a lie long enough, it becomes the truth". This describes what happened to me in a way because the more people treated me like garbage and repeatedly told me that I was worthless, a piece of dirt, garbage, a fat piece of shit, etc. the more I believed it. It was possible to shake it off at first, but after having it pounded into me over and over again it started to sink in. Had it been one or two people doing this to me then I don't believe I would have accepted it, but when it seemed like everybody was treating me this way then it was very hard to refute. My fragile self-image/self-worth started believing everything, and in my eyes I actually was that horrible person they made me out to be.

It should be no surprise that during this time, my weight issues grew (both physically and emotionally). Since I never went out and spent most of my time at home, food was the only constant thing in my life. I ate and ate and ate anything that was around. My weight went up and I got more out of shape than I had ever been. As a result, my clothes did not fit too well and I was petrified to go clothes shopping and buy new clothes. I would try to stretch my clothes as big as I could in order to prevent having to buy anything new and bigger. Even though I stretched my clothes, they did not fit right and I was constantly reminded of how big I was as clothes would pull tight in certain places and accentuate certain places on my body. This caused my self-esteem to decline even more and caused the teasing and tormenting to remain at a heightened level. Once again I found myself being depressed about my appearance and the torment I received as a result, but found that I still turned to food to relieve me of the pain.

I also had a hard time watching my brother and sister at this time. My brother and I have totally different personalities (people cannot see how we are brothers) and he had a much easier time adjusting to life in Wall. He had many friends, played many sports, and was popular among his peers. He has a way about him that allows him to get along and speak with everybody, and also has the ability to make everybody fall in love with and be around him. I am still very jealous of Jason for these things. My sister also had many friends. I resented this about them. I wanted what they had, but I could not get it. This added to the pain I was feeling. I felt like I had no control over anything in my life. I could not get the friends I wanted. I could not stop the pain. I could not stand up for myself. I could not stop eating. I couldn't even go through with killing myself. I had no control over anything, and I hated it.

It is very hard for me to think back to those years and reminisce on all the shit that my life was made of. Occasionally I will ramble to my wife about what had happened, but I do not like talking about it at all. There are also songs and movies and even smells that I hate because I associate them with that period of my life. I can't even look at chicken fingers and tator tots without thinking back to that time because that was the lunch on my first day in that school. I cannot hear certain songs that I listened to during that time without thinking back to the way my life was when those melodies first came about. I often hear people talk about being scarred. I can truly say that I am a very scarred individual, both physically and emotionally.

Senior year was different than the three previous ones. My "leave me alone, stay away" attitude seemed to draw people to me. People now wanted to hang out with me. It was a whirlwind time for me. I still did not let anybody get close to me because there was no way that I could trust them after what had happened. I never grew to trust more than one or two people from this time, but made it through senior year and the summer that followed.

Monmouth University was supposed to be different than high school. People were supposed to be grown up and all the childish bullshit was supposed to be gone. I moved into Cedar Hall with eight other guys. My second roommate and I were close at first, but things changed and I found myself being the brunt of some of the torment that I had experienced in high school, by him and his friends. It was nothing new to me. It was the same old stuff and I knew how to react to it. I wanted it to end, but I could not get myself to confront him about it. I had no confidence in myself. It was me versus all of them, and I believed that I did not stand a chance. It was just easier for me to suck it up, internalize it, build that wall even stronger, and deal with it.

At Monmouth I became extremely close to a girl named Amy that I had met a few times during high school. She and I had an excellent friendship since day one at Monmouth. She even introduced me to my future wife. She commuted to school the first semester and after much discussion decided to move on campus in the spring semester. This was great for me. I thought this was a way for me to get out of my room and hang out with a person who I thought was my friend and could trust like no other. I also thought I could possibly make some new friends as well. I found myself spending a considerable amount of time in her room and we had a very close-knit group of friends that did everything together. I'd say that there was probably 10-12 of us and we went to the movies together, went to restaurants, went to clubs, went to the beach at 2 in the morning, and just hung out together. For the first time in a very long time I had that sense of camaraderie that I felt on my freshman football team. I felt like I belonged, and that life was good. I adopted the role of the protector. Because of my size, I felt that I was the group's bodyguard (especially for Amy). Over the course of the semester, Amy had a crush on a member of our group. He was a complete asshole and would often do stuff that I knew would hurt her and others around me. There were a few instances where he made fun of another girl in our group to the point where he made her cry. He not only verbally abused her but he also physically abused her. She had bad knees and he would kick out the back of her legs and make her fall. He was a cocky asshole that was bullying my friend, and I hated bullies. I tried to protect my friends and confronted Amy about him, which turned out to be a fatal mistake. Within the course of a week or two, I found myself being ostracized by most of the group. The girl that I had trusted and befriended to the highest level had turned on me and spread lies throughout our clique and urged most of them to turn their backs on me. She said that I stole from them, that I talked bad about them behind their backs, and that I was a horrible person. This did major damage to me psychologically. I thought the pain was over. I thought that I was in the clear, and now I felt myself right back to freshman year in high school. The ones that I had grown to trust had left me to mentally rot, and they could not care in the slightest. I was all by myself again, with a shattered self-image. I made it through the last two or so weeks of the semester all alone in a very depressed state.

During the two semesters of my freshman year, especially the second one, I found myself eating large amounts of pizza, French fries, Chinese food, burgers, etc. and drinking large amounts of beer, thus putting on 10-20lbs. I did not feel as bad as I normally would have because I felt like I was around friends, but once my world came crashing down, I felt horrible and had considerable emotional pain caused by my weight. To make matters worse, academically I finished my freshman year with a cumulative GPA of 3.3. This was very good in comparison to most of the other freshman that I knew, but at home I found that it was not acceptable. My parents expected more from me. They wanted me to be better because I was the "smart one". I left my freshman year fatter, friendless, broken, feeling worthless, and feeling like I had disappointed my parents. I left angry, upset, untrusting, and inverted even more.

Later that summer I began dating my future wife, Lindsey, and entered my sophomore year at Monmouth. This time I got along with all of the people in my suite. I still felt insecure about myself because I was so big and everybody else was very outgoing, had charm and charisma, and most importantly they were skinny or athletic. I can remember one of my suitemates saying to me "Vic, you would be so much more intimidating if you were a few inches taller". This statement, although innocent in his mind, did not do much to better my self-image. The fall and half of the spring semester were normal. I was eating all of the junk food the dining hall and local fast food/delivery restaurants had to offer. I found a place called Nelly's that sold "fat sandwiches" and I would eat them nonstop. I would order a "Fat Night" or a "Fat AXP", which was a sandwich with a cheese steak, chicken fingers, onion rings, mozzarella sticks, tomato sauce and French or curly fries respectively on it. I would easily eat mine and then eat half of Lindsey's. I would eat tons of Ming Ying's General Tso's chicken, Tony's $5 large pizza, cheese steaks, chicken cheese steaks, fries, curly fries, etc. I ate and drank A LOT, and ended up being close to 290lbs. Also during this time I felt pressure from my parents to get my grades up. The fall semester ended with me receiving a 3.85 GPA and even though I had received praise for this, I felt pressured to do better. I felt like the message to me was "A 3.85 is good, but a 4.0 is better and that's what you should be getting". I put myself on a mission to do better.

The dominos were all lined up because of everything that had happened to me during the first 19 years of my life, and were just waiting for something to push that first one over. Finally something pushed the first one over one day in the first week of March of 2002 as I was in the dining hall with some of my suitemates. I was standing in the grill line like any other day, probably going to order a cheese steak and fries when all of a sudden out of the blue I said "fuck it, I'm going on a diet". This wasn't the usual "I'm going on a diet" thought. It was quite the contrary. A switch had been flicked, seemingly meaningless and without rhyme or reason. It was completely out of the blue with no prior thoughts or planning to help in my decision. It was a switch that would set certain things in motion which would engulf every aspect of my life for the next 6 years. From that moment on I seemed to have declared war on food and decided to take control of my body. My diet had severely and drastically changed at that exact moment. Timing is everything and this was not the best time for this to happen because a major fad was about to explode in America. This was at the very beginning of the "carbohydrates are bad" kick in the United States so I easily convinced myself that carbohydrates were bad and I had to cut them out of my diet to make myself be the person that would make me happy. I heard the hype all over the television and internet. I took a big look at what my diet consisted of before the switch was flipped and noticed a very common trend: all the food I was eating was high in carbohydrates. It was so easy to accept the correlation between what my body was like and what I was eating. Thus, the way to turn things around both physically and emotionally was to cut those "bad" carbohydrates out. Now, when I say cut them out, I literally mean that I "had to" and therefore succeeded in cutting out all carbohydrates out of my diet. I had decided I was going to eat nothing but protein. In reality when this "diet" first began I ate almost nothing. A few pieces of grilled chicken, maybe some cheese. That was it. No grains, no milk, no flour, no fruit, and no oils. They were "bad". My caloric intake was down to almost nothing and I began exercising in my room. I didn't really know how to exercise so I started running in place when my roommate was in class. I would hide it from everybody because I was ashamed of it. Weight began to drop off, but I did not know how much because I was still wearing the same clothes as I had before. I was at school seven days a week and had no scale to weigh myself on. All I knew was that something was working, and I wasn't going to quit. A consequence of my lack of eating and use of exercise was that my blood sugar would drop suddenly and my Seratonin levels would be out of whack, which caused severe mood swings. I would go from happy to depressed or happy to moody/angry in the blink of an eye, but as time went on I found those happy moments to be less and less prevalent. I would also feel the physical effects of having such low sugar as I would have constant headaches and had difficulty moving, walking, talking, and concentrating. Carbohydrates serve as the body's main source of fuel and by eliminating them from my diet I was basically starving my body, my organs, and my brain of the fuel it needed. This made it hard to meet the standards that I had internally set for myself in terms of my schoolwork, but

I was determined to fight through it. I eventually fought my way to the end of the semester with a 4.0 GPA and went home to hear some praise from my parents and praise from people that had noticed my weight loss.

I avoided the scale for my entire life. I hated seeing how high my weight was so I would make any excuse known to man not to get on a scale and dreaded it when a doctor or even worse, the school had to weigh me. Once I moved back home for the summer, however, I had access to a scale on a daily basis as well as exercise machines. I began running on the treadmill in the basement and lifting weights on a daily basis as well. It was difficult at first because I had not run like this in my entire life. I did not know the mechanics of how to run properly so I felt a considerable amount of pain in my legs and knees especially since I was running without any shoes on. I did not care how difficult or painful it was. For the first time in my life, I became infatuated with exercising, and exercising a lot. I would run until I couldn't run anymore and lifted as many weights as I could. People would give me advice on how to bulk up and get the most out of weight training, but putting on muscle and becoming "ripped" was never my intention. My only intention was to burn as many calories as I could. All of a sudden I found myself getting on the scale a few times each day. As I stated earlier, I feared the scale my whole life, but now seeing the number on the scale was a necessity to my life. I wanted to make sure that every time I weighed myself it was lower than my previous weigh-in and if it wasn't then I would panic, exercise more, and cut out a meal or two. Even though I was exercising to such a high level, I was not eating much at all. A few thin pieces of chicken breast, an ounce or two of cheese, and not much more a day was my intake. I was easily burning 3-4 times what I was taking in each day, and I felt it because my sugar levels made me feel miserable. I was very irritable and would easily snap at anybody that questioned what I was doing. I hated the way I felt and the way I acted half the time, but I kept seeing the pounds burn away and my clothes getting looser so I kept on going. I became extremely obsessed with getting as much weight off of my body as possible. I started seeing 5-10lbs coming off each week and I was "loving" it. One's body is the only thing in life that he or she can really control and I thought this was my way of finally controlling the image that the world saw. I decided that I was never going to be fat again. I was never going to be the fat, insecure kid standing there in his underwear again. I felt like I had total control over my body, and everything else for that matter, for the first time in my life. People kept telling me; "Wow you look great, keep it up!" and this made me feel wonderful. It made me feel like all the hard work was truly worth it. Positive reinforcement was the only thing that fed me during this time because there certainly was no food feeding me. Reinforcement fed that which was driving me to do these things. Reinforcement was everything that "it" needed to sink "its" claws in and convince me to continue with what I was doing. My relationship with Lindsey, my girlfriend, suffered. She did not understand the mood swings and we would fight quite easily when they would occur. I started to isolate and push everybody, including Lindsey out of my life. There was a period after a fight that we had, when I was so psychologically fucked up that I did everything I could think of to have Lin break up with me. I felt that she had betrayed my trust and was going to hurt me so I tried to end the relationship before she could hurt me like everyone else had. I would snap at a moments notice, be mean, refuse to talk, or hang out. At my worst, I refused to touch her for over a month. I considered her to be one of "them" and she could not be trusted. It was a bad situation, but she stuck around (Lord only knows why, but I'm so happy that she did). In addition to Lindsey, I started pushing family members and people from school even further away. It seemed like the only person I wanted in my life was "me" because the only person that I could truly trust was "me".

Since starting the diet, my target weight had always been 180lbs. I hit that number quite easily, but once I was there I was not satisfied. Because I had lost a considerable amount of weight already I had extra skin in some areas of my body and had stretch marks all over my body. My body distortion was horrible, as I did not see myself in the mirror as looking skinny. I saw fat, so I decided to keep going. My target weight and the scale were lying to me because whenever I looked in the mirror or saw my shadow, I saw otherwise. I kept on pace: 175lbs-172lbs-170lbs-165lbs... I just kept going. I went back to school for my junior year and barely ate when I was on campus. I remember people seeing me for the first time and asking me if I was sick. The change was that drastic, that fast. The only food I kept in my room was a tub of mixed nuts and some canned chicken. These lay under my bed for months. I just didn't want to eat. I saw what I saw and felt the way that I felt in my body so I wanted to go lower and lower and nothing was going to stop me. I was in control no matter what people said. I would take long walks around campus, going up and down as many stairs as I could find, and running on the university's track nightly. My food intake dropped more and more. I quickly started loving the feeling of an empty stomach as compared to the feeling of having food in me. An empty stomach was so comforting to me, it was the only way I knew that I could absolutely prevent weight gain. Food in my stomach meant that fat could come back. I began to fear that if I ate then I would gain back the 120-130 lbs that I spent the last 6 months losing. I remember living on very little sustenance, and would panic when I put the little bit of food in me that I did. I would "feel" the food in me and instantly feel myself getting fat again. Do not forget that I was not consuming ANY carbohydrates at all, thus I was not giving my body any of the fuel that it needs to operate. The mood swings were a constant thing and I felt horrible both physically and mentally due to the lack of fuel, but I found a way to persevere. The feelings that I experienced when my blood sugar and Seratonin dropped were horrible. The world would be in a daze. It became incredibly hard to think a clear, logical thought and was very hard to remember almost anything. I have an impeccable memory but couldn't remember things that happened twenty minutes prior. It was hard to see, and very hard to hold myself up when I was standing. It took much effort to get up or even move. I would experience dizzy spells once I did anything. I had horrible headaches that made my mood worse. Also, I had a hard time speaking (in a way other than my stutter). My speech would be slurred. It seemed like my tongue did not want to work and my lips would not move right. This would happen constantly for the next few years. It was hell, pure hell. My relationship with my girlfriend went through a roller coaster ride during this time as I became increasingly obsessed with not eating anything and doing anything to burn off what I had eaten. She had no idea that anything was wrong with me. Come to think of it I didn't think anything was wrong either. In her mind I was just on a hardcore diet and fitness kick and was basically just being an asshole most of the time.

I began bingeing around this time. Our dining hall had a grill, which is where I ordered roughly 99%

of my food from but once I came back for my junior with my new look and diet agenda it was switched to a "serve yourself" grill. There was no longer any kind of line that I had to stand on and there wasn't any limit to the amount of food I could take. I would eat the exact same foods every day but some days I would eat much more than others. There were times where I would eat three pounds or more of hamburgers, chicken, cheese, etc. I would polish off one plate and then go fill my plate again and maybe even again. I believe events like this happened because my body was so starved that I became ravenous when "safe" foods were around and could not control myself. I would feel all right as I was eating, but once I was finished there was a drastic change in the way I felt. After these binges I would panic and try to figure out a way to burn it off. I would instantly feel the excessive amount of food in me and think about nothing except for what was in my stomach and the "fact" that I was going to go back to 290lbs as a result. I would restrict later in the day and figure out any way to do some exercise. The binges that I experienced during this time and the ones in the years to come made my relationship with food an even more adversarial. I was bingeing on the exact same foods that I ate everyday, thus making those foods "unsafe". I was not bingeing on chocolate cake or candy. No, I was bingeing on chicken, burgers, cheese, which were the only foods I permitted myself to eat in my day-to-day life. Basically I was reminded of the emotions connected to my binges every time I sat down for a meal.

Somewhere along the way I lost the control I thought I had (maybe I never had it). I also made sure that I filled myself with large amounts of water each day. I became obsessed with my water intake and it became a compulsive behavior. It was at a point that if I did not have crystal clear urine then I would force myself to drink more. I made sure that I had a certain amount of ounces during each class and would basically gorge myself later in the day. I convinced myself that this was healthy and that I was flushing only bad things out of me. In reality, I was doing things that were making my situation even worse. First, I was filling my stomach with large amounts of water at a single time, thus fooling my body into thinking that it was full. I would tell myself that I could not possibly be hungry because my stomach seemed full. At the same time, however, feeling large amounts of water weight in me would send me into a panic for hours to come. It made me not want to eat anymore than I already did because I felt extremely fat as it was. Second, I probably was urinating all of the nutrients out of the blood going to my brain. It made thinking and functioning even harder than it already was. I felt horrible and angry from what I was doing to myself, but feared that if I ate something I would gain weight and become the fat kid in his underwear again. I also felt horrible because of the pressure that my parents and I had put on myself to get a perfect GPA again. The work was not easy, and my brain was working on overdrive to try to get it done. I had to fight through it just to concentrate, but I had fought through things in the past and I was going to come out on top this time. Earning the grades that I did is very impressive, but what makes it more impressive to me is the fact that I was able to accomplish it while being in the condition I was in.

We had a blizzard in 2003, and I got snowed in at school. I was in my room for 3-4 days straight with little or no food. When I ate the food that I had, I would panic. I vividly remember being in there with two or three cans of chicken breast and a tub of mixed nuts. I would go insane if I ate a handful of nuts. After I finished the homework I had, I began writing song lyrics. I began writing about the demons or the monster within me that caused me to feel the way that I did and made me do the things that I did. The words coming out of my fingertips started to scare me. I began realizing that "the monster" controlled my thoughts and my actions. I couldn't escape its grasp. It was the first time that I had really thought about what was going on in me. I kept these lyrics hidden on my computer.

Time passed with little change. My life would go up and down and the fears would overcome me more at some times than others, but I lived for years with a constant fear that if I ate I would gain weight. When I would eat, I felt it necessary to get on the treadmill or lift weights until I felt that I had burned off every calorie that had been ingested and then some. At certain family functions where large amounts of food were present that I would normally eat, I found myself going on uncontrollable eating binges. This would often happen when my Nana would cook me an entire turkey breast and put it in front of me. I would eat the whole thing and then three pounds of cheese, then sausage, then hamburgers, then chicken, then nuts and anything else that was there. I could and would literally eat an entire cheese platter and then want to get 5 burgers down. I would eat and eat and eat, even when I knew that I did not want eat to anymore. Once I was done, I would immediately feel fat and start trying to figure out what I had to do to lose what I just put in me. I would spend the next day running 5-6-7-8 miles (and then not eat much of anything) to try to purge the food through exercise to make weight gain impossible. I would still see myself as being fat and hated eating.

These binges would happen frequently at family parties or over my parents/grandparents house. I would make sure that I would run a few miles the morning of the party in anticipation of not being able to control my eating and then be right back on the treadmill the next morning. I would beg them not to order cheese platters or a lot of food for me, but they did not listen because they did not understand. They just wanted me to eat something. To them the best thing for me was to eat a lot, but this was actually causing me much distress and harm. The binges made me depressed. I would feel great while eating, but then I would get depressed immediately after I was done because I would start worrying about gaining weight. I had no control over stopping my binges and I had no control over exercising after my binges were done. It totally consumed my life. I could not stop. I had no control. I exercised like a mad man and stuffed sugar-free candies down my throat because of their laxative effect. The combination of eating so much and the candies caused me extreme stomach discomfort the next day, a feeling that I dreaded. At times I would hate eating all together. This depressed me because I was starving and afraid of eating and then when I ate I would be upset because I had eaten. It is very interesting that at times I refused to eat a drop of anything and at other times I could not stop myself from eating.

I stopped going out to eat because I felt I could not trust the cooks. I thought they would cook my food with things that would make me gain weight. I also hated going out to eat because, more often than not, the chefs or waiters would screw up my order or not cook it to my liking. There is nothing like the feeling of sitting at dinner with a group of people and watching them all gorge themselves with appetizers and all this good food, then the little bit of food that you order comes to the table and it isn't any good. The fears ran my life to the point that I would not let people cook for me at all. I had to bring my own food and cook for myself to make sure that I had control over what I ate. I feared eating. I feared bingeing. I feared gaining weight. I feared being depressed. I feared being looked down upon. I feared what people were going to say to me. I feared other people knowing my situation. I feared what I was going to have to do to myself to make sure that I didn't gain weight.

I ended up being very structured with the way that I operated my life. I had my way of doing things regarding food and exercise and I was not changing them for anything or anybody. The best way for me to illustrate this is to actually map out a typical week in my life. My days would go one of three ways:

1) On Monday, Wednesday, and Friday: I would eat an Atkins brand protein bar for breakfast, do a heavy workout using weights in the gym during my lunch hour at work, eat about one pound of ground chicken and broccoli for lunch, eat another Atkins brand protein bar for a snack, go home and sneak in a 2,000 pushups, 1,500–2,000 sit-ups, and chin-ups, eat another pound of ground chicken and broccoli for dinner, and finally have some sugar-free candy as a dessert.

2) On Tuesday, Thursday, and Saturday: I would wake up 5 o'clock in the morning to drive to the office and

run on the treadmill for 75 continuous minutes as fast as I could, eat an Atkins brand protein bar for breakfast, work out the other muscles that I missed the day prior, eat about a pound of ground chicken or turkey and broccoli for lunch, go home, do 1,000 triceps dips, eat about a pound of ground chicken or turkey and broccoli for dinner, have some sugar free candy for dessert.

3) On the days that I was up at school for my masters courses I would bring 4 or 5 Atkins brand protein bars with me, which was the only food I would eat for the 8-9 hours I was on campus. On campus, I would intentionally walk up and down stairs, walk across campus, and find any way possible to burn some calories during the free time I had away from my homework, studying, or researching.

Those were my weeks and there was very little variation from them. I might have thrown in some ground beef here and some cheese there but for the most part that was my schedule, and that was how it was going to be. If anybody tried to change it I would panic and try to figure out ways around it. This went on every day for 3-4 years.

Other than eating the same things everyday, I would eat many things in the exact same way everyday. I later found out that these are called food rituals. I would literally eat my sugar-free candies and protein bars in the same way every time I had them. I got very distressed if anybody tried to change it. I would pick little pieces off of the food at a time and eat each piece very slowly, savoring every little bit of it and prolonging the experience. It would literally take me an hour and a half to two hours to eat a protein bar, and a half an hour to eat one little piece of sugar-free toffee. By prolonging it, I seemed to trick my body into thinking that it was eating much more than it really was.

Physically, I really destroyed my body due to the excessive amounts of exercise I was doing and the lack of food that I was taking in. My cardiovascular exercises were devastating both physically and mentally. Before I would start running on the treadmill for my 75 minute run, I would be dreading it. I was so physically exhausted that I didn't want to do it, but it didn't really feel like I had a choice. Why? Every single time I ran, the first ten minutes were miserable. I had no fuel to run on and those first ten minutes were always a very hard hill for me to climb. Sometimes after those first ten minutes I would set myself on cruise control and make it on pure adrenaline, but other times I had to push myself somehow for the entire 75 minutes. Those specific times I was running on "fumes" and had to push through the severe physical and mental exhaustion. Unfortunately, those times seemed to become more prevalent as time went on. I was not going to be happy until that 75 minute mark hit, and definitely would not be happy until the calorie meter on the machine reset. There was also a period where I was using an elliptical machine instead of a treadmill. Once again I set the 75 minute mark for myself on this machine. On this specific machine, there was a gauge that went up and down depending on how fast you were going. Once I discovered this, I did not let myself get below a "10" at certain points or below an "8" at other points. The mission was to go as fast and as hard as possible for the entire time. It was just as intense and hard as the treadmill. I believe it was on this machine that I developed my obsession with the calorie meter resetting. I was elated the first time I did it, but once I had done it one time then it was "required" that I had to do it every time. This meant that if at the 75 minute mark arrived and I did not see 0000 on the calorie meter then I was going to keep going until it happened. I also took full advantage of different stair cases that I encountered everyday, especially the one in the townhouse that I was living in at the time. I would start at the top and run down and then run right back up, and would repeat this 10-15 times at any given moment.

I worked as a stagehand at the Meadowlands Sports Complex in East Rutherford, NJ for about 6 years. I was obsessed with my weight and food and activity for 5 of those years. The job was great as I got to build stages and productions for hundreds of major concerts and shows such as the Rolling Stones, the WWE, U2, Bon Jovi, Bruce Springsteen, Metallica, Madonna, etc. The work was very hard, backbreaking work at times and I was wearing myself down further by doing it to the level I was doing it at. It was more than work to me, it was a way to burn calories. Work usually began somewhere between 6am-8am and the day wouldn't officially be over until well into the morning hours of the next day. I would load and unload trucks, build stage decks, set up barricades, and then ultimately take it all down. When a show was in the stadium I would be there days in advance to help build the major scaffolding that is required for such shows. Those days were an average of 12-16 hours of straight work, and were mostly done in the blistering sun that the June, July, and August months bring. I would usually bring a protein bar or two with me and use that as some food, and occasionally I would find some cold cuts in the catering area to eat but other than that the only thing fueling me was black coffee. It was the only thing keeping me from passing out and dropping from exhaustion and it gave me the "strength" that I needed. When I would occasionally find food I would allow myself to eat, I would go on a minor binge and then obsess and it for the rest of the day, thus pushing my body even further than I already was in these situations. When I think about it now, I was seriously putting my life and the lives of everyone around me in danger. My head wasn't always clear and it was very hard to concentrate on what I was doing thus I could have made a mistake and either severely hurt or killed myself or someone else.

I would panic and have much anxiety when my daily routine changed due to one circumstance or another. Usually I would react by changing the amount of food that I would consume, always in a negative way. If, for some reason, I was not going to be doing my normal amount of exercise or had someplace to go, then I would just restrict what I put into my body. The rationale behind this was simple: the less activity I did, the less calories I burned, thus I had to eat less calories. The problem was that I did this to such an extreme that it was putting me in a dangerous place medically. I can think of two specific occurrences that stand out to me regarding these behaviors. First, I was in the weight room one afternoon, and while bench pressing I was hit with a case of vertigo. It was pretty debilitating, but I actually forced myself to finish my workout and get my weight training in. When I was finished I just sat in a chair and told people that I could not move. I was driven home and spent the next 24 hours on my couch unable to move one bit. The next day I collapsed on the floor of the bathroom and had to be carried out on a stretcher and taken to the hospital. It turned out I had one of the worst vertigo cases they had ever seen. The only thing I could do for the next few months was just lay on the couch. I would be home alone from 7a.m. to about 8p.m. Monday thru Friday with only my mind to keep me company. Here my rationale of "doing less exercise means consuming fewer calories" hit full force. I literally ate no more than 600-800 calories a day for the two months I was home. All the muscle I had basically evaporated off of me and I withered away to nothing. Every time I did eat something, the thoughts would immediately surface and drive me insane for hours. Apart from the thoughts I had when I ate something, my depression got much worse during this time. I was in total misery both physically and mentally.

The second occurrence was when I was stricken with major pains in both my hips, which caused considerable pain all day, every day. This was obviously the result of the exercise I was doing, and it got to the point where it was getting very hard to walk. I went to see an orthopedic doctor who sent me to physical therapy. My physical therapist had me doing little exercises and stretches to help with the pains, but I was ordered not to do any other exercises. So, once again I knew that I had to reduce the amount of calories being burned. Of course, once I heard that I had to reduce the amount of calories I could work off I just decided to reduce my caloric intake altogether. I took advantage however, of the exercises he had me do and started to use them to burn calories rather than fixing my hips. This went on for 2 months of physical therapy and for a few months afterward because the pain would not go away. What it all boils down to was that I was finding any little way to restrict my calories.

My pulse rate was very low, about 40 beats per minute. I know this because I used to count the number of times my heart would beat in a given minute. For some reason I convinced myself that the slower I could get my pulse, the better shape I was in. I would mentally freak out if all of a sudden my heart would start beating in a "fast" manner. During my heavier years, I had very high blood pressure, which was so high that many doctors feared that I would have a stroke at a very early age. Once I dropped the weight, I tried to get my blood pressure as low as I possibly could. I correlated a higher blood pressure with being fat and out of shape, thus I wanted to get the farthest away from this and get my blood pressure as far away from the point it was when I was heavy. The top number of an average blood pressure is 120, but I would not be happy unless that number was 70 or 80.

As a result of having a pulse and blood pressure at such low numbers I would get extremely dizzy at random points, especially when I stood up. I would lose my balance and need to hold onto something to steady myself.

I had major knee problems with one of my knees when I was in my heavier years, but the wear and tear that I caused as a result of my exercising further devastated the original knee injury and caused major problems in the other one. There was a period when I was running on the treadmill without any footgear, thus there was nothing to protect my knees from the impact. There would be considerable knee pain in both knees before, during, and especially after each exercise session and soon the pain lasted all day, every day. I was in so much pain, but there was nothing that was going to stop me from burning my calories. The bones began rubbing against each other and there would be constant painful cracking with every movement. I eventually had to wear two knee braces on each knee just to workout. My legs were also getting inflamed on a regular basis. It seemed as though the pain would start in the knees and then drift up into my thighs and resonate there all day. I also ended up with bursitis in both of my hips. I deal with this leg pain on a regular basis even today, and it is a daily reminder of what I did to myself. Other than destroying my legs I really hurt my rotator cuff in my left shoulder. The amount of weight training, pushups, triceps dips, and pull ups that I did virtually wore it out. I remember hearing it crack and feeling a burst of pain during each push up and each pull up. The pain was intense but once again let me say that nothing was going to prevent me from performing my exercises. I convinced myself that pain was ONLY a four-letter word.

Also, from years of using ritualistic behaviors while eating the protein bars and sugar-free candies I have ground crevices in my front teeth. I would put each little piece of food in between my top front two teeth and my bottom four teeth and basically grind it down, but after doing this for so long I began grinding my teeth down. I can actually put a fingernail into each tooth because there are little "valleys" in each tooth.

It should be noted that during this time that my body was not expelling waste in a normal way. There would easily be one to two weeks in between my bowel movements. I was not eating any fruits, vegetables, or grains so there was nothing being ingested to aid my body with this, plus I was eating cheese and fatty foods that were basically clogging me up. My consumption of sugar-free candies was not helping in this matter because they tore up my stomach and gave me incredible pain but never really had the laxative effect that I intended for them to have on me. I was incredibly constipated and occasionally had bloody stools, but I did not care one bit. A very close person to me died right in front of my eyes of colon cancer and I remember saying to myself that I'm probably heading in the same direction, but I didn't care. I didn't care because I didn't care if I died or not. As a result of being so clogged up I began partaking in PICA behaviors. Somewhere along the way I convinced myself that human hair must be loaded with fiber so I started plucking and eating my own hair. I would pluck bunches of hairs from my head, from my arms, from my chest and eat them. I would try to pluck them out by the root so I could bite the root off. Thinking back to it now, it sounds very disgusting to me but this is what I did to try to clear myself out and in some other occasions I did this to fill myself up.

I found myself depressed because of what I did to myself: low blood sugar, achy knees and legs due to over exercising, fear, unorthodox behaviors, etc., but I also found myself becoming depressed because of what the people around me said to me. People did not understand that I was not doing this to myself on purpose. I did not see myself as being emaciated, but I know that I probably was. I knew that I was too skinny, and I knew that I was hurting myself. I was not doing this on purpose, but people thought that I was. It is very hard when people came to me and said "you are too skinny, you have to eat something, stop doing this to yourself". They did not understand that it is not as easy as just eating something for me. I was at war with myself. I would have liked to eat more and be healthy but my brain said no. Eating a plate of macaroni was not the simple solution that everyone thought it was. I often found myself extremely depressed when confronted by family and friends with these statements. It hurt me that they thought that it was so simple to turn around. When people told me this stuff and told me what to eat I created a defense strategy of just laughing it off and not showing that it bothered me, but it really did.

I grew to hate being around people because I was afraid of what they were going to say to me. I avoided going to any and all social events because I did not like being around people. This was extremely difficult because the people that cared about me the most were the ones that were hurting me. They did not understand what I was going through and they did not understand the mood swings, so fighting occurred because I did not want them to know the secret I was holding inside of me. I was very ashamed of my secret.

I thought I was an extremely strong person, but I was afraid and worried that people would see me as having a "girl's disease".

The way to prevent any more pain than is necessary was to keep this secret to myself, and so I did for a very long time. I was in denial that anything was wrong for so long, but I knew deep down that I had a problem. The hardest thing about the whole situation was the fact that I was going through this hell all by myself. Nobody but me knew what was going on. I could not bear telling any of them and made sure that none of them had much more than a suspicion as to what was going on. Accompanying these feelings was my lack of wanting to do anything. I had no drive to do the things that I would normally like to do. Lindsey would have loved to go out and do things, but I had no drive or desire. I just wanted to stay home in my comfortable environment with my usual surroundings and foods. I didn't want to be placed anywhere that I did not know, or in a situation where I'd be uncomfortable.

My Monster Within

Over the years I have felt like I have had little or no control over my life. I know my parents mean the best for me, but I feel as though they are pressuring me to do things that I may not want to. I feel in college that a 4.0 GPA is expected (and demanded) of me and that I would be disappointing them, and not good enough for them if I do not achieve it. I really wanted to become a chef and go to culinary school, but it was not allowed because "I was too smart to do that", and was ultimately swayed away from the idea. I feel like I am being forced to go to law school, I feel like I am being forced to follow a path that is being laid out for me without any regard for the way I feel. When I do express my feelings, they are often brushed off to the side and ignored. People tell me that I cannot waste my talents and that I am being guided and given the tools needed so that I may have a successful life. I guess I am just supposed to listen to the people who try to give me the tools to succeed in life. I feel that most of my life is dedicated to living up to the expectations that everybody else has built up for me. When I attempted to regain some control over certain things in my life, such as requesting that my family not have a cheese platter, or asking for things to be done in certain ways, I was often called difficult because I had too many "rules". It made me feel like I was the bad guy when all I was trying to do was feel a little better and relieve some of the stress. This wore me down. My "rules" were just a way for me to gain some control over minor details in my life, and when I was called difficult, it depressed me to the point that I wanted to be left alone by the world. I emotionally broke down while driving home one day because I was told that I had too many rules and was difficult because I wanted a hair trimmer. I was recently married and was not happy about anything. My wife and I would fight about stupid shit because she did not know what was going through my mind. I felt horrible for what I did to her. What makes me sad is that I couldn't even fight my problems on our wedding day and honeymoon. I was mostly able to suppress the feelings, but I went on a small binge at our fucking wedding reception. These were supposed to be the greatest and worry-free days of my life and I had to fight the thoughts in my head. We also had a wedding party a few months later and I could not push myself to have a bit of my own wedding cake. This is something I truly regret.

My days at work were miserable. Putting my body through what I was doing to it was physically wearing me down, and all the mental anguish I was going through was mentally wearing me down. I hated life. It was as simple as that. I would easily slip into a deep depression during my workdays. Any little trigger would set me off. I would sit in my chair, not say a word to anybody, not smile, and just get lost in my disordered thoughts ruminating all day. People would try to make me laugh but I wouldn't give them the time of day. Life was miserable, I was miserable. To cope with my feelings I would run up and down the stairs or try to do any little bit of exercise possible to make myself better, but this would ultimately make me feel worse. The restricting and exercising were my methods to numb me to the pain I was feeling. They were my ways of controlling my feelings. In reality, those two methods were accentuating my depression so I started to drink alcohol as a way to further numb me out. My wife used to call my drinks "Vic drinks" because of the extreme amount of alcohol I would put in each drink. I would take a 16-ounce glass, pour tequila, rum, or whiskey into the glass until it was ¾ of the way full and then put a splash of diet soda in it for some flavor, or I would just drink straight whiskey. I would drink one, pour another, drink it, and usually pour and drink another. When I would drink, one of two things would happen to me. I would either get relaxed, carefree, and somewhat happy, or I would sink even further into a depression. When the latter happened I would be miserable and sit just there lost in my head, ready to jump out the window. The depression, unfortunately, happened much more than the happiness. It seemed like none of the ways I used to numb myself out helped in a productive way, and ultimately caused me to sink further and further into my depression and into my eating disorder.

I finally made the decision to tell someone what was going on in my life. I was on the treadmill during my lunch hour and decided that I was going to tell my mother. I went into a trance for the thirty-five minutes that I was running and basically scripted out the conversation that I was going to have with her. I was going to tell her, and maybe things would get better. I got off the treadmill and went to the phone. I dialed the number and waited for someone to answer...nobody did. I hung up and decided that maybe I should not tell. The door that had been opened was now closing. The next night when I was at my parents' house I binged on rib eye steaks and grilled chicken and ended up going home an emotional mess. Once again the thought of telling someone popped into my head, but that door was still slowly closing. Then the following Monday, my dad called me and asked me what was wrong (actually, he pried it out of me). "This is it!" I thought to myself. Maybe I can tell someone now. After some debate I decided to tell him the next day. He picked me up and we drove to the Stewart's Restaurant in Point Pleasant.

After much anxiety I told him what was going on. I remember sitting there shaking and fighting back any tears that I felt welling up in my eyes. It was an extremely uncomfortable situation, but I knew that I had to do it. He said he thought there was a problem. He was happy that I was asking for help, and promised to get me help. The funny thing about the whole situation was that I was confessing that I had an eating disorder to someone that was stuffing hot dogs, fries, and a root beer down his throat.

Later that night I took Lindsey up to the garden at Monmouth University (the place where we got married) and told her. Her reaction was simple, "Ok, I'm here for you. Let's get you better". My dad called around to different specialists and he took me to see a psychologist in Central NJ. I started seeing Dr. E. and was immediately diagnosed with anorexia nervosa. I remember being so scared before we met with him because I was going to have to bear my soul to a stranger. The three of us sat there and discussed my situation and then the doctor interviewed me alone. He

was easily able to realize what was going on.
Physically I was about 60% into my disorder, which is
not so bad considering what I had put my body through.
Mentally, however, I was 95%. I was very mentally
fucked up. He wrote my diagnosis up on a sheet of
paper. I went home to open my *Diagnostic and
Statistical Manual for Psychological Disorders* and
went to "307.10" (the official diagnosis number). Once
I saw it in the book, it finally hit me that I had a REAL
problem. Now I had a name for what was wrong with
me and was not imagining all of this. I was now
officially an anorexic and I could no longer deny
anything. I sat there and read the diagnostic criteria for
the disease and saw my life on the pages. The
diagnostic criteria for the disorder consist of:

> A)   Refusal to maintain a body weight at
> or above a minimally normal weight
> for age and height (e.g., weight loss
> leading to maintenance of body
> weight less than 85% of that
> expected; or failure to make expected

weight gain during period of growth, leading to body weight less than 85% of that expected);

B) Intense fear of gaining weight or becoming fat, even though underweight;

C) Disturbance in the way in which one's body weight or shape is experienced, undue influence of body weight or shape on self-evaluation, or denial of the seriousness of the current low body weight.

Once I read these words I found some meaning to my life and understanding for why I felt the way I did, but it also scared me to no end. From that day on I was set up with Dr. E as my psychological counselor and a woman named "H" as my nutritionist. I saw them both once a week and things were going decently. I took a body metabolic rate test to see my caloric needs while resting and active. My resting rate required me to eat at least 1400 calories a day to not lose any weight and my active rate was about 2400-2500 calories. The sad thing was that I was probably eating around 1000 calories at that point (400 less than what my resting minimum was). Also what scared me was the fact that the person administering my tests became alarmed when my heart rate jumped fifteen notches when I had to stand up. She was ready to put me in the hospital if it rose any higher.

All I want[1] is a little control of my life. I do not like the blank stares that I can feel myself giving the world. I do not like being in a war with myself. I do not like worrying and fearing the essential things in life. I am getting help now, and I can finally see a trickle of light at the end of the long, dark tunnel. I just worry that the soothing light at the end of the tunnel is just a freight train coming my way. My support group is there. My wife right now is the greatest thing in my life. She helps me and tries to be my crutch when I need one. She understands it all and is willing to take

---

[1] The remainder of this section is written in the present tense because this is how I originally wrote it. It was how I felt at that exact moment in time.

on the baggage that I have dropped at her door, and I am forever thankful for it. My parents and siblings are there for me, even though they do not truly understand all of it. It is totally new for them and they are trying to learn as much as possible to help get me through this.

I now have a security net for the first time in a very long time and it feels good. It feels good that I am not alone now in my quest to overcome the monster. It feels great that I do not have to keep this a total secret. I understand that I have a psychological disease, and I am very lucky that I decided to take charge and try to regain control over my life. This disease has the highest mortality rate of any psychological disorder and I refuse to make myself another statistic.

Part II

From this point on, I am writing about 3 months after the preceding was written (It was written late August and it is now late November)[2]. Life has changed in some ways and remained the same in many other ways. First off, let me explain what has changed. The first major change, and in my opinion the most important, is the fact that I feel that my safety net of people around me have a greater understanding about the disease and will do anything for me. My parents have become so accepting, helpful, and supportive that it is a total joy to be around them (most of the time). No longer do I feel like I have to be "on guard" around them and give into things just to make things easier on them or just not to hear any type of complaining. They are there for me whenever I need it. I can call them and we are very open with each other, which makes

---

[2] There will be times in this section where I speak in the present tense because I discuss feelings/events that were happening at the time I wrote this section. I wanted to keep this book as raw as possible and I feel it allows the reader to see how I was both mentally and physically at that point. When I switch to past tense I am discussing events that happened prior to this writing.

everything much easier on me. They have a better understanding of my "rules" and do not call me "difficult" or anything like that when I ask for things done in certain ways. They have somewhat of an understanding why I do a lot of things now and things have been a little easier as a result.

Besides relationships with both of my parents improving, I also took a major step by bringing two new people into my net. The first person is "L". I had wanted to tell her for a very long time, but felt uncomfortable and scared about making more people aware of my situation. I didn't want to put her under any pressure. Once again, I was trying not to make other people's lives difficult. One day as I left my nutritionist I decided to call her, and I'm happy that I did. After disclosing my secret she disclosed to me that she had battled an eating disorder for two decades. We had a wonderful talk and it is great knowing that I have someone close to me that knows exactly what I am going through. I have someone to call when I am having a problem and she has someone to call if she needs to. The other person is Nana. I was very hesitant about telling her what I was going through. I had long debates with myself as to whether or not I should let her know. In the end, though, I did not want to hear the: "I wish you would just eat", "Why aren't you eating", "You worry me", "Why do you want to be so skinny", "Just gain some weight" statements that I had been hearing nonstop for the past few years. It is very wearing to hear it over and over again and very hard to think that people believe I am doing this to myself on purpose. I wanted Nana not just to stop saying those things to me, but I wanted her to know that I am sick, that I am not doing this to myself, and that I need her help. I can remember the expression change in her face as I told her and watched the shock and fear come into her eyes. She was very scared, and rightfully so. After I told her, I could tell she was very worried about me. By her knowing, though, she has made life easier for me when in family situations. I am extremely happy with my current situation with my family.

I have declared myself independent from my eating disorder. I realized that it is not truly a part of me. It is not Vic, it is a separate entity that hops in the driver's seat and whispers in my ear. This demon or monster is not me. It is not Victor Avon. It is mainly just a parasite that has jumped into my system and has sucked the life out of me.

Psychologically, I have improved, but I really have not at the same time. Dr. E. was able to dabble into my psyche and show how past events and pressures, which I have discussed earlier, have been the things most to blame for my problems. I have a much better understanding of the disease that I battle and have gone through great lengths to overcome most of the depression that I used to feel. Through my visits with Dr. E., I have been able to come to terms with my depressed moods. He, in a way, has given me the key to unlock all the emotions and feelings that were running my life and making it miserable. And, he has shown me a way to cope with them in a manner that allows me to live my life. I remember when I first began treatment, my emotions were going ballistic on me. I am not a very emotional person, and it was a very emotional time for me. I would cry and break down very easily. I hated it. My emotional life was a whirlwind. I remember when my parents threw Lindsey and I a wedding party at their house, and there were close to 200 people there. I was so afraid that people would see me and make a comment to me or something along those lines. Even if they did not make a comment directly to me, I was worried what they may have been thinking of me. I was so afraid that I did not even want to go to my own party. A few people made comments to Lindsey but nothing was said to me. I remember going on a small binge at that party, but it is the last time I remember going on any type of binge. Unfortunately, I ended up purging everything out of me later that night and next morning (not of my own choosing because I drank too much and had gotten sick).

He was also able to put a name on something that I constantly did in my head. He told me that I was

like a cow that was chewing the cud. I obsessively
ruminate on a constant basis. If I am hungry and know
that I need to eat something I will sit there and fight
with myself for hours on end about eating whatever it
is. Let me explain what I mean, by illustrating an
example of this:

I need to eat and want to eat a piece of a
protein bar. I will have the following debate in my
head: "I really should eat, but if I eat then I'll be
depressed, but I know that I should eat, I might feel
bad, maybe I really don't have to eat, no I really should
eat, but I am worried that I am going to have to work
off what I ate, but its hard to think/move and I have a
headache, but I will be worn out after I eat".

That may go on for five minutes, or may go on
for a few hours. I eventually give in and eat what I
debated eating and then the debate continues:

"Wow, why did I eat that, what am I going to do
to burn that off, I feel like shit, I don't want to work
out, but I have to burn it off, but if I work it off I will
feel like shit, but if I don't work it off then I will feel

like shit, I just want this to stop, I really need to go running, why am I so worthless".

The debate would go on for hours and hours and I'd end up depressed and moody if I ate or if I did not eat. It is a no win situation. Other than my depression, I also have been told that I may have (a slight case of) obsessive-compulsive disorder. At times I have urges that I must exercise or be active and I cannot fight them. If I do fight them, I become depressed. These impulses are extremely strong and I cannot fight them. Someone seems to be in the driver's seat and pushes the exercise/become active button and I must listen or else. I really am fucked up.

It is important for me to note that I have made some improvement with the food I take in. I began eating bread on a regular basis (a lower carbohydrate bread), and have started eating fruit. I began by eating baby food and have worked up to eating solid fruit (apples, pears, and pumpkin so far). These were small steps to average people but major steps for me. I had to psych myself up before I ate that first baby food as I listened to some music to get me ready for it. My food intake, however, really is not as good as it should be. With all that being said however, life is still very hard for me. I have every intention of getting better and listening to my nutritionist and everyone around me to eat more and to try more things, but every time I make a step forward, I take two steps back. Whenever I take a giant leap (such as eating some fruit or some bread) I ultimately cut my intake of everything else, thus eating the same or less amount of calories everyday. I cut out the extra protein bar, which has 260 calories, because I had eaten an apple, which had less than 100 calories. I cut the full 1 pound of chicken or beef for dinner to about half a pound, simply because I had eaten two pieces of bread with my lunch. Mentally, I was "conquering" the fear of eating new foods, but calorie-wise I was failing because my intake was being lessened. I felt that because I had eaten newer, carbohydrate-filled things then I must reduce other calorie filled foods to make sure that I did not gain weight. I was feeling better, in terms of my thoughts and my moods, but I was wearing myself out physically. Even when I knew that I should eat more to compensate for the fewer calories, the disorder would tap me on my shoulder or whisper on my ear and fuck everything up. I would, for instance, eat a container of baby food that had some blueberries and apples in it and then be worried afterward and not eat as much as I should. The panic that I was so used to would set in. It would say things like "You shouldn't eat that extra piece of protein bar or handful of peanuts because you ate an apple and some bread for lunch. Do you remember what happened back when you used to eat stuff like this in the past? You were 290lbs, you were nothing, and you will be 290lbs and nothing if you start eating again! You are special now, you have control, there is nothing wrong with you now, this is what you always wanted to be, do not blow it, listen to me, Vic!"

I remember one instance where my nutritionist weighed me and told me that I had gained one pound. One pound! I thought it was the greatest news. I was so happy that I was getting through this thing once and for all, and I even went home, told Lindsey and we took a shot in celebration. This joy only lasted the night. The whispering in the ear and the panic began the next day. "One pound will lead to gaining it all back, you will lose control of your body and self if you keep this up", is what the disorder was telling me. And I believed it. The incident set me back at least a week or two. I had reverted back to old habits making sure that I lost that pound (and maybe some more in the mean time). I still have no idea as to what I weigh. I never wanted to know once I started treatment. After the "one pound" incident I told the nutritionist that I do not want to know how much I weighed, nor if I had gained any weight from my last visit from now on. I did this to make sure that I did not have any more panics. I just assumed I was doing well instead of being told if I actually was or wasn't. Logically, I know not to listen to all of this, but I just can't stop. I am being worn down to the point where I just do not care anymore. I am tired, tired of fighting with myself, tired of the conflict, tired of "chewing the cud" (obsessively ruminating), tired of debating with myself as to whether I should eat or not, tired of rationalizing that what I had eaten (or not eaten for that matter) was proper, tired of my obsessive compulsive impulses to exercises, and just tired of the bullshit.

I have reached the point where I really do not care about whether I live or die anymore. Fighting for so long has taken its toll on me and has really made life very unattractive. Why would I want to go through life constantly fighting the demon inside of me? To me, it may be more attractive to pass on and let it all stop, then there will be no more suffering, there will be no more pain (for me that is). It crossed my mind that maybe there is no afterlife, maybe this is it, but if that were true I still would have no more pain. I want to make it perfectly clear that I would not kill myself. I won't overdose on some medication, cut my writs, or pull the trigger. I do not want to have to do that to myself, nor do I want any of my loved ones to know that I had done such a thing to myself. On the other hand, I would not mind if God just took me. I often find myself speaking out loud as I walk the garbage to the dumpster asking God to please take me tonight, please end my suffering. The thought does not bother me that I may go to sleep tonight and not wake up tomorrow.

Besides not caring about life anymore, I lost my faith. I was very religious, and attended church on a regular basis, each Sunday at 10am. As the suffering got worse and worse over the past few months I started to doubt that there is a God or that he cared about me. If He were there then why would he do such a thing to me? I did nothing wrong in my life, I am not a bad person, and I do not deserve this. There are many assholes and pieces of shit in this world that have life by the balls and live in the lap of luxury, and I am suffering every day. It just makes me question everything that I once believed in. Why me? I have done nothing to anybody…never have…and I have been suffering for so long and have been tested and fucked with for most of my life. I have lived through all of these tests but am growing tired of them. The only thing that people tell me when I explain my feelings is that "God works in mysterious ways" and "this will make you stronger". These answers are not good enough. They do not help me in the slightest. I am looking for some insight and nobody is able to give me any. If I am supposed to believe that an imaginary man in the sky created me and loves me to no end then I need Him to show me something to help me along. I am very agnostic and very doubtful that any such God exists. I have seen too much pain to believe that anybody created me and loves me.

I recently read a book entitled *Life as a Male Anorexic*. It was the only book I could find about the male perspective of anorexia written by a male anorexic. Everything that I read or view on the Internet has been done for girls or from a girl's point of view. This gets me very angry because it seems like everything out there is for a girl, totally following the stigma that it's a girl's disease. How could I relate to a girl and a girl's emotions? I can't! So I was very happy that I was able to find something written by a man. It was a tragic story told by Michael, who battled for many years and never benefited from any treatment. While reading the book I found myself relating to many of the things he felt/said. I read about his depression, about his lack of drive, about the struggles in his head, and it made me feel for the first time that I wasn't the only man that felt this way. I felt a bond with Michael as he constantly discussed how he hated that everybody would not let him get better at his own speed. It all had to be rushed. I can relate to this. There are many times that I feel that everybody wants this to be fixed at a faster rate than I am comfortable with. I wish they would just allow me to do things at my own pace, wait until I am ready to go from step 2 to step 3, and not try to already be on step 5. If I am not emotionally and physically ready then it will cause me much stress. Ultimately I will resist and it will not work. I saw the exact same sentiments in Michael's book. A good example of this is with my nutritionist. She is well meaning (I think), but I went into one of my last meetings and was very excited to tell her that I started eating solid apples and was eating pumpkin (major leaps for me). Lindsey and my family were so proud of me the second they saw that I had improved (I can still see the smile on Lin's face). I thought "H" would be so proud, so happy for me, but it was just like "O.K. good, now how about some sweet potatoes?" I couldn't believe it, I had just conquered this major thing and she wanted me to jump into sweet potatoes...FUCKING SWEET POTATOES! I knew this was not going to end up well, and I ended up bullshitting her and telling her that I would try when I knew there was no way I was ready for it. Personally, I think my nutritionist is a good person. She is very nice and I think she cares, but I hate going to her. It seems like nothing is ever good enough for her. I feel like she is constantly pressuring me to do more and more when I am not mentally ready for it. She keeps pushing and I keep resisting. She was never 290lbs and she never had an eating disorder. She doesn't know that it isn't that easy for me to listen to her. I hate seeing her and wish I could just solely see my therapist. She also looks like someone that I would not ever want to be like. Her hair and skin looks worn or tattered and she looks like a hippie, not something I aspire to look like. I'd rather look like a skeleton than look like her.

Michael also had a similar outlook on life and death as I do, as I have discussed previously. He ran away from his parents and his treatment facilities and attempted to starve himself to death a few times, one thing I never even considered doing. In his final epilogue he states that he decided that he was going to starve himself to death. He had reached that point where he was finished with the struggle. His final statement made a major impact on me because it summed up the way I feel about life. He said, "I don't really want to die; it's just that I have no desire to live". Michael died on October 9, 1997, three days after writing these last few sentences. A very common theme in his book was that he repeatedly spoke negatively about treatment of any kind and recovery in general. The more I read, the more I started to be convinced that what he said was the truth, and accept the fact that treatment would probably not work for me.

The only thing that I still hold on to in life is the thought of what it would do to my family and, more importantly, to my wife if I left them. They are the only bits of life that I am holding on to. They have been my safety net these last few months. They are doing all that they can to try to make me feel better. They have tried to pick me up when I am down. They truly care. I mentioned earlier how my relationship with my parents has improved ten fold, but what I have learned about my wife truly amazes me everyday. She truly is the greatest thing to happen to me. She did not sign up for this, but she cares for me more than I thought anybody could. She protects me in every situation, deals with me when I am depressed or shut down, listens to me when I am babbling on about life, and does anything I ask her to do, or not to do. She puts me ahead of herself, something that I never wanted her to do. She is number one in my life, but I always want to her put herself ahead of me in her life. She really is a blessing, an angel that I was lucky enough to be blessed with. I love her with all my heart and I do not want to hurt her by leaving her. I may bring peace to myself, but I will leave behind misery to everybody else. I really do not know what to do. I guess I will just keep on living this horrible life. I have never been a selfish person, but maybe it is time for me to do what I feel is best for me and not everyone else.

Part III

I had finally hit a very low point. After almost four months of therapy and nutritional counseling, nothing had really changed, and I was still a wreck inside. I was still afraid to eat my little jars of baby food or my little containers of tuna. It is quite sad when I think that a grown man was afraid to eat baby food. These little tiny containers that you feed to a newborn child would not hurt me, but the disorder would whisper in my ear and make my rational thoughts go away and be taken over by my panics and fears. Nothing much changed when I started eating solid fruits either. I would still limit the food prior to eating and after eating that apple or pear. I must state that the first time I ate a solid piece of fruit was not because I wanted to, but rather it was out of desperation. I thought I was dying. It was on our vacation to the Atlantis Resort. Both Lindsey and I got sick and could not eat as much as we should have, but this brought back old habits of mine. We would go and go and go and go all day, all the while not eating very much.

Thinking back to it I was probably walking about 4-6 miles a day and operating on MAYBE 800 calories. Anyway, one day I was by the pool when my chest started hurting and my body felt weird, like it had never felt before. I thought, "Shit something is not right here, I think I am dying! I can't die on our vacation! What can I eat? Let's try an apple." So I went and got my apple (which I have to admit was quite delicious). I find it funny that I was not willing to try an apple until I thought I was going to die. I wasn't worried about dying, however. I was just worried about dying on my first vacation with my wife in another country. I just wanted to make it home and then we'd see what happened. For the rest of the vacation and the week following, I was back to old habits and totally restricting my food. I saw how much I could do on so little calories and embraced the idea that I did not have to eat because I had just done what I did in Atlantis without food. Two weeks later is when I began eating solid apples and carrots regularly and the pumpkin, but I had the fears all the same.

My Monster Within

My days at work were very hectic and action packed. It would be non-stop from eight o'clock in the morning until 4:30 in the afternoon. This was both good and bad. Good because it kept me busy and my mind occupied so that I could not slip into any kind of depression or think too much. And it prevented me from doing any unwanted exercise. It was bad, however, because I would be going a mile a minute and had tremendous stress that flowed through my body. All of this was happening on only a "Morning Start" bar in the morning before work, and a toasted tuna sandwich sometime between noon and two o'clock. Other than that I was not eating much. The stress of the days took their toll on my physically. I would get bad anxiety, the kind that causes pain from the middle of the back all the way through the body to the center of the chest. It hurt and bothered me, but I had to get my job done. I was going to make sure that my department would not flounder, and everything would go smoothly. When I would get home, I would be pretty tired and "pick" on food until dinner. Picking meant half a protein bar or a piece of candy and an apple before my dinner, which was usually around 8 o'clock or so. At this point I really was asking God to take me. I wanted my suffering to end. I did not want to fight anymore. It would sadden everyone around me, but if they only knew the constant never-ending struggle maybe they would understand my point. It seemed like my entire life was consumed by how I was going to make work better and how much I didn't want to be here anymore.

Last week, Lindsey and I had a session with Dr. E. and I could tell that he was very concerned about me. He dropped a bomb while he was speaking to the two of us. He told me that I had lost 5lbs since I was at my heaviest while being in the program. I was a little bothered by this, but not much at all. Lindsey however, panicked at the news. I could see it in her face as soon as he said it. She was so concerned on the ride home that her words came out in anger and told me that I had to tell my parents. She explained that 5lbs to me is like 20lbs to a normal person and that she was worried that I was going to die and had to tell my parents. She gave me an ultimatum that if I did not tell them, then she would. While she was yelling at me and pleading with me, I never lashed back. I just sat there and drove the car and was seemingly unaffected by what she was saying. I did not fight because I had no leg to stand on in the situation and I totally knew where she was coming from, but I wasn't concerned or worried or saddened in the least. The next few days of work went by as hectic and stressful as the last few. Every time I spoke with Lindsey she would ask if I told my parents and I would say that I had not. I really didn't want to tell my parents because I did not want to worry them, and didn't want to disappoint them.

Then one day I went into work about an hour early to get some stuff done before a meeting I was having that day. I worked my ass off that day and even decided to stay late to finish up some work. I called my parents and Lindsey at five o'clock to tell them I was staying late and they all told me to go home, but I assured them all that I wasn't going to stay much past six and that I needed to get stuff done. I was getting a ton of work done, all the while feeling major stress and anxiety, and decided to call Lin and see how her drive was going. I called and she did not answer, and I called a few minutes later and no answer. I knew exactly what was going on. She was talking to my parents. In my head I said "Thank You, Baby" because I did not want to tell my parents, but I wanted her to do it for me. Sure enough on my next call she answered and told me that she was talking to them on the other line. I finished up what I was working on by 6:10 and packed up and left. On my drive home I got a call from my dad who was very upset to the point where he was crying hysterically and pleading with me to change what I was doing. By the end of the conversation I promised him that I would change, a promise that I did truly mean and would do (I thought). I went to work the next morning ready for another day, when my phone paged me and someone told me to come downstairs. It was 8:15 and I thought that it couldn't be my dad because he never comes in, especially this early. Sure enough it was him, and he was distraught. He sat me down and talked with me for an hour or so, all the while crying his eyes out with this look of fear in his eyes. It was the first time in my life that I had seen him in such a state. He assured me that if anything happened to me and I ended up dying that he would probably kill himself because he would feel that he didn't do everything possible to help me. He also pounded the idea that my mother's life would be over as well as my grandparents', brother's, sister's, and wife's. Their lives would be over, whether emotionally or actually, if I lost mine. The odd thing was that I was watching all this happen and I knew it was a sad moment, but I was totally unaffected emotionally by the situation (much like when Lin was pleading with me in the car). It was like I was totally detached from everything that was going on. It seemed like I really did not care what was going on. I was very close to rock bottom. The one thing that had kept me going all this time was my emotions, and they felt like they were dead.

We took a ride in his truck for a few minutes when one of my uncles called him and ironically wanted to talk to him about my health. I then made a major decision, one that I would never have considered in the past. I told him that I wanted to sit down with all my uncles and tell them. We were going to meet at Billy's house and as I walked up to the house I was basically trembling. I was so afraid of what they were going to think or say. When we sat around the table I made my dad do all the talking because I was too afraid to do it. Through the tears, he was able to explain much and stuck up for me when people would ask the "Why don't" or "Why can't" questions. I chimed in every now and then to further explain some of the points that I felt they needed to hear. All in all I was surprised by how the conversation went, in terms of their openness and willingness to listen. They wanted to understand. It was amazing and made me feel like I shouldn't be holding this in as a secret anymore. Everybody backed me in the conversation and kept telling me that if I did not want to live for me right now then I had to live for my family and loved ones. I accepted the point and decided that I was going to do that for them.

Everybody, though, wanted me to be hospitalized for a month or so. I did not want to go away, especially because that meant being away from Lindsey for our first Christmas and New Years as a married couple. Right then and there I decided that I would basically submit to my dad and do whatever he and my family wanted me to do to get better. If they were the ones that were worrying and didn't want me to die then it was up to them to make sure that I didn't. I called up Lindsey and asked her to come home from work early because we all had to have a family meeting.

We all met up at my house and I watched as my mom, dad, wife, and sister distressed about what to do about me. Dad was yelling because he was worried, which caused everyone to argue at one point or another. But what I sensed from everyone was that they were all very concerned about me. I watched all of this happen, still very unemotional (much like a psychopath), and wasn't moved in the slightest. I wasn't even moved when we added up the calories I eat on a day-to-day basis and found it to be around 1000. We decided to go to the doctor's for a physical and blood work so dad and Lin rushed me there. I told the doctor everything, without any hesitation because since telling my uncles earlier that day I really did not care if anybody else knew. The doctor was concerned and checked me out. He sent me for blood work to see how my organs were functioning, and an echocardiogram to make sure that my heart was not giving out. He also prescribed me an antidepressant, which he said would help me with my moods and anxiety. What stuck with me the most was the fact that he was very empathetic toward the situation. It seemed like he cared, which made me more willing to open up to him.

After we left the doctor, the three of us went up to see the nutritionist and Dr. E. On the ride up my dad told me that I was "fired" for a week and had to stay away from work to make sure that I didn't have the stress on me. I kind of embraced the idea because I knew that I needed some time to recover a little. We also decided that instead of hospitalizing me we would put me on the Zone diet where my food for the day is going to be delivered each day. A certain calorie range is picked out for me and all I have to do is eat what comes in my little pouch everyday. Since I really didn't give a shit any more I said "fuck it" I'll do whatever you want me to do. We first saw the nutritionist, and Lin and my dad got to see her for the first time. I think they saw her the same way that I did. She seemed lukewarm to the Zone idea, but saw how headstrong my dad was and didn't put up much of a fight. My dad did not like her and her philosophy with things, and the two butted heads a little bit. I just sat there totally detached still while this was all going on. During this conversation I asked for the first time in a few years how much I weighed. Since it was a day of new beginnings, I wanted to see exactly where I was at so I couldn't pretend everything was all right and I couldn't be in denial of my weight. I started the program at 149lbs. I went up to 150lbs (my one pound weight gain), and since then it had been a slow decline to the point where I was at 145lbs. I never thought that I would be that low. I figured I was in the 160s but never 145lbs! It was shocking news but I wasn't shocked. I was still unemotional (it was very odd).

We then saw Dr. E and he was amazed at what happened that day. He couldn't believe what had transpired and was happy. He also embraced the Zone idea because he had two patients that were doing it. Once I learned that, I was immediately more optimistic about the Zone because people in my situation were using it and they "enjoy" it. The meeting went well and by the time it was over and we were in the car I was pretty tired. I had been through a shit load that day. I watched my loved ones cry and plead, told my uncles everything, handed my life over, went to the doctors, got on antidepressants, and accepted to be on the Zone. I cannot believe what I had done in one day.

The next morning I went to get my blood work done. The funny thing was that I had to fast for 10 hours before I gave the blood so I joked with my dad that here we are trying to eat more and I have to fast now. I gave the blood and decided that I was going to start eating then and there. I made him take me to the food store where I bought whole wheat Lean Pockets for breakfast, a Smart Ones pizza for lunch, and a Lean Cuisine for dinner. As soon as we got home I cooked up the Lean Pocket and ate it. The weird thing was that I ate it without any care in the world. I was still unemotional, but I was also unemotional about the food I was putting into me. My dad watched as I ate that stupid pocket (which was ham and cheese, and I HATE HAM!) and he was elated. A few hours later I at the pizza in front of my mother this time and she was just as pleased as he was. Then for dinner, I ate the Lean Cuisine in front of Lindsey. They were all so happy for what I had done that day. By the time dinner came around I was emotional for about 15 minutes prior to eating and a little bit of panic was setting in. I told Lindsey that I did not want to eat it, but she told me that I had to. I was able to tell the feelings to fuck off and sucked down the dinner. By the time the day was over I had put three actual meals into my body for the first time in 4 or so years and had more carbohydrates in me than I had since March of 2002. It was a big day to say the least. The next few days passed with pretty much the same thing happening. I was eating more, and the antidepressants were helping me. My calorie intake was up to about 1300-1400 or so, which was a major deal for me especially because I was eating breads, mashed potatoes, corn, beans, peas, rice, and other things that I had banned from my life in the past. There have been a few times since everything started that I have been a little resistant to eating more and have resisted things people told me to do, but for the most part I followed along. The old fears were still there in little drips and drabs, but nothing like they were the week prior. My dad was very pushy with making sure that I ate, which was very overbearing, but he was doing what he thought was best. Sometimes I ate when he told me and sometimes I didn't, but I saw that it was getting easier than it was in the past. Overall I was still very unemotional with the whole thing, which may be a good thing considering the major changes I was going through. I think much of that was due to the antidepressants, and I was very grateful for that. The following day I was going to start with the Zone eating program, something that I was looking forward to and somewhat fearing at the same time. We started me out at 1500 calories a day and then moved me to 1750, 2000, and so forth.

Hitting this low point may have been the best thing for me. By not giving a shit about whether I lived or died I allowed myself to be guided by the ones that want me still around. Yes, if I die then my suffering will be over, but the suffering for those around me would be paramount. I have to go on for them, but I cannot do it alone. I can't trust myself to do it for me. I have already tried that I it did not work. Just like Dante I need them there. I need buddies to take me by the hand and help me climb out of hell. There are going to be times when I am slipping back down the crevasses and I need them to catch me and bring me back. I cannot explain how happy Lindsey's phone call to my parents made me. I believe that without it, I may have been dead with a few weeks. I was putting myself under so much stress, eating very little, and not wanting to live. It was a formula for disaster. The phone call not only helped me with that but it also gave me a new outlook on life. I used to be very ashamed of my disease because I was a man with a "girl's" disease, but now I go through my days with the motto, "Yeah I'm an anorexic and you can go fuck yourself if you have a problem with it!" I don't give a shit about what people think about my disease now. I have told a bunch of people since telling my uncles and do not have a problem at all with it.

Part IV

I am adding[3] this section on February 13, 2007, over two months since the last section was written. I have been on the zone meal plan since that period and actually "enjoy" eating the food. Looking back, I find it amazing that I was able to almost immediately eat the majority the food that was presented to me. I would cheat every now and then, but I'd say that overall I would eat 95% of the food. My mood was pretty good during this time. I began taking my antidepressant, which really helped me with the depressed moods and the anxiety. The only side effects were some bad cottonmouth and sleepiness, but I think I'll take those two over depression any day.

Something happened to my body that really scared everybody around me because I began eating actual food. My mother, father and I were sitting in

---

[3] There will be times in this section where I speak in the present tense because I discuss feelings/events that were happening at the time I wrote this section. I wanted to keep this book as raw as possible and I feel it allows the reader to see how I was both mentally and physically at that point. When I switch to past tense I am discussing events that happened prior to this writing.

with Dr. E. and he warned us that my body's metabolism might kick-start soon and that I would begin losing weight. Up until that point I had been gaining a pound and a half to two pounds a week and was on track to be where I wanted to be. That morning I weighed in at 147lbs. My dad asked me to get on the scale the next day because he had just bought a new electronic scale and wanted to test it out. I could see the shock on his face when I stepped on. I was 139lbs! There is no way that this could be. We went and got dumbbells from the gym to check the calibration, and were amazed to see that it was accurate. I had lost 8lbs in less than 24 hours, and my dad was freaking out. He panicked and got the doctor right on the phone. Dr. E. assured us that my metabolism had jumpstarted and that I needed to add more calories to my diet…a lot more calories. I wasn't ready to hear this. I had come so far and had achieved so much that and now they wanted me to increase twofold. I knew that there was no way that I was going to be able to add 1200 calories they wanted me to add overnight. I did not restrict my diet in any way after this all started, but I did resist including new things into my diet. I was very resistant and butted heads with my father because I felt as though I was being forced to go too fast and thought that he felt that I was losing weight on purpose. For the next few days I would get on the scale secretly each morning and watch it go from 139-138-136-135lbs. Wow, I was six feet tall and I was 135lbs, which was pretty hard to believe. It was scary but at the same time it was exactly all that I wanted to see. I was eating everything and still losing weight. It was great for the eating disorder part of my psyche.

For the next few weeks I would play a little game with myself. Half of me wanted to gain weight and get better and the other half loved being at the 135lbs that I had become. I'd go up a few pounds and then back down a few. I saw myself as a Chinese ying-yang, a circle that is composed of interlocking black and white halves. The black half was my disorder and the white was the side of me that wanted to get better. It was quite an interesting combination, but a very real combination. At the time of this writing, however, I finally said "enough is enough". I was in the process of planning my future and was two weeks from closing on a house that Lin and I bought. I ate more every day and was getting on the scale every two days to see if my two-week experiment was truly worth it. Life may be worth living after all. That's a feeling that I had not experienced in such a long time.

My life is changing, hopefully for the better. I know that I have a long road still ahead. I know I am not even close to be being fixed and that I will never be truly cured of this disease, but I can see now for the first time that maybe there is some light at the end of this tunnel. At this moment I am living life for everyone else, but maybe that is the best thing for me because it really gives me a reason to live. In the *Inferno*, Dante had to experience the different rings of hell, each one worse than the other. I feel like I have been in hell for so long and have gone through the different rings, but one thing that I have to remember is that in the end Dante walks out of hell.

Part V

It is[4] the beginning of March of 2008, over one calendar year since my last writing, and I am adding this from the inpatient lounge of the Eating Disorder Program of the Medical Center at Princeton. As you can probably surmise, things have not gone especially well for me. In March of 2007 I was let go by Dr. E. He saw that I had been eating the Zone meals and had been improving. We started to taper off on our meetings, and one day he told me that he would contact me in a few weeks to follow up and set up another meeting (this is a topic I will get back to later). Everything seemed to go well the months following Dr. E's "release". Lindsey and I bought our house in Brick, NJ and were very happy. It seemed like I was comfortable eating things and was eager to get off of the Zone plan so that I could try eating like a "normal"

---

[4] There will be times in this section where I speak in the present tense because I discuss feelings/events that were happening at the time I wrote this section. I wanted to keep this book as raw as possible and I feel it allows the reader to see how I was both mentally and physically at that point. When I switch to past tense I am discussing events that happened prior to this writing.

person. One day in March I decided to cancel my meal plan and surprise Lindsey one night by taking her out to dinner. I remember being so excited and could not wait to drop the bomb and to see her reaction. We went to the Monmouth Mall and as I was driving out of the parking lot I pulled into the parking lot of the Chili's restaurant. She thought that I had made a wrong turn until I pulled into a spot, put the car in park, and got out. Her reaction was exactly what I had hoped it would be: shock, awe, excitement, and joy. She lit up with emotions and we went inside and ate our first dinner together in a very long time. It was a very special night for both of us.

Over the next few months we ate together and I may have had a slip up or two, but everybody was there to make sure I did not fall back to the state I was in. I began eating "junk food" again. Lin and I would go to the Rainbow Diner and I would order a big Reuben sandwich with French fries, cole slaw, and a pickle. We would go to the Chinese restaurant around the corner and get chicken with garlic sauce, fried rice, egg rolls, etc. I was eating and did not have many ill feelings toward it. I was putting on weight. I fought my way from 135lbs up to 155lbs. I thought things were on the up and up and that I was done with my ordeal, or at least able to control it. I got promoted within Avon Contractors. I jumped at the opportunity to become a project manager after someone had been fired. It was very hard and stressful work but it opened doors for me within the company and also meant more money in my paycheck each week. Lindsey also got a new job at Rutgers University and was going to make about $20,000 more than her other job at Rider University. We were living a pretty stress free life.

Then suddenly, that soothing light that was at the end of my tunnel turned into a freight train coming my way. Things got very rough for me around September of 2007. A few of the old feelings would pop into my head and my disorder would knock on my shoulder every now and then, more frequently than in the past. As I look at it now, I felt as though I had separated myself from the disorder, but in reality I only put it in the closet for a period of time. As I look back at it now, during that summer I was not really better with my eating. Sure, I was eating more things and eating "junk foods" but I was being very active around the house and doing much physical yard work while not eating during the day. The reason I would not eat during the day was because I knew subconsciously that Lin and I would be eating big meals together later. I don't believe I was aware of my behaviors at the time but looking back it is quite easy for me to see that my disorder was still controlling my actions and decisions. There was nothing normal about what I was doing. My old friend was lying in the shadows waiting for the right moment to pop out. It would open the door every now and then and have its way with me, but I was usually able to keep it hidden away. In September, I started having nightmares at night. This really freaked me out. I would have recurring dreams that I would be gaining weight and no matter what I did to prevent it, I would still gain more weight. In my dreams, I was feeling and living the fear I once had. If I ate, I would gain all of my weight back and be unable to stop myself. They were very vivid, and felt all too real. Needless to say, the dreams really scared me and turned the key on the lock that I thought I was able to keep safely closed.

Shortly after the dreams began, my dog Angel, got mysteriously sick and the veterinarian could not find what was the matter with her. I watched her get sicker and sicker each day as she did not eat, did not have any life in her, and did not want to do anything. She reminded me of how I used to be. She could not walk up steps, so I would have to carry her. We finally had to check her into the Garden State Veterinary Associates Hospital and keep her there for a few days. I was lost without her. This dog is everything to me. She is my best friend and the one living thing on this Earth that I have truly felt will never ever hurt me. She is usually right there by my side for 20-22 hours of the day, and knowing that she was very sick and may not make it out of the hospital was a horribly helpless feeling. I would try things such as sleeping on the floor next to her bed just to feel close to her. I was a wreck over this whole thing. The dominoes were beginning to line up again and very shortly they would be pushed over.

After picking Angel up from her four-day stay at the hospital, we took her home and tried to do everything the hospital said that we should do to try and get her well again. She came home as a mere skeleton of what she had been. You could see every bone in her body. The week that she came home, Lindsey woke up one morning for work and could not walk. She had been struck with a case of vertigo. The vertigo, however, was very severe and basically incapacitated her from doing just about anything. She couldn't drive, work, or even walk. She was basically bedridden. We went to every doctor we could, to try and figure out the cause. Nobody could tell us anything. It was very scary because some doctors told us it might be something with her brain and could be very serious. Now, I had to deal with a dog that I thought was dying and a wife that may be dying as well. The stressors were growing and there was nothing that I could do.

Lindsey could not do anything for four months except just sit on the couch at home and try to recuperate. Because she had been in her probationary period at Rutgers, she lost her job, cutting our household income virtually in half. This meant that I had to pick up the slack from the financial loss as well as worry nonstop about my two sick ladies. I felt helpless. I felt that I had no control over these major things that were happening in my life. Also, things were extremely hard for me at work. I did not receive the proper training or direction for the role I was promoted to and easily felt overwhelmed when things started to get busy for the company. All of a sudden I was in charge of fifteen million dollars worth of projects and had no real direction. I tried to remedy this situation early on by asking for help from my boss, but my requests and pleas seemed to have fallen on deaf ears. For the first time in my life I was actually asking for help with something and I wasn't getting it. I interpreted the response I got as if my opinions didn't matter. I felt that my boss' workout sessions in the gym were more important than anything I had to say. As a result, more and more stuff was thrown on me and my continued cries for help were basically thrown into the wastebasket. I was admitting that I was overwhelmed and falling behind, but my boss was quick to tell me that I was doing things wrong and that I had better fix things "NOW". It certainly was not an easy time, and my disorder took advantage of my weakened state. There really was nothing I could do. I had to be strong because everything else in my life was falling apart. I had to try to gain some sort of control in my life. This is where I resorted back to old behaviors. I began by controlling the only thing in my life that I could. I started restricting myself by slowly cutting down our diner and Chinese trips. I would then cut out other things here and there. I was reestablishing my old habits in a major way. It was so easy to do it because I would use excuses such as "we need to save money". I was under so much stress that I really did not want to eat anything at all. I did not want to show what I was feeling because I did not want my wife to see that the stress affected me as much as it did. I just locked it all up and internalized it like I had done in the past. My eating disorder would tell me to restrict and I listened because it was the only way I could think of to cope with the emotions that I was dealing with. My depression was slowly growing at this time as well. I would be "down" for most of the day, and was having a very hard time getting my responsibilities done at work. I once again disconnected from most of the people in my life and lost most interest in doing things that I liked to do. The people around me saw that something was happening again but I constantly assured them that I had control of my situation and that I was ok. I think I kept telling myself that I had my disorder in check. I realize now that I knew all along and was just in a state of denial. I felt like I was sliding back down the mountain that I had once climbed, and I was sliding fast. I was once again headed in the direction of not caring whether I lived or died.

I feel it is time that I address Lindsey's parents and the strain they have put on our relationship and the progression of my disorder. I bring this up now because they have been a major part of my regression over the past few months and one of the reasons that I am in the hospital. Lindsey's family and I do not have a relationship in my eyes. They have done things to Lindsey and myself that no family should ever do to a daughter and her husband. I have always had a problem with many of the things they represent and things they do, but I never took it out on them or was ever disrespectful to them. Her father "R" worked for Avon Contractors, my father's construction company, as the family handyman. When I found this out, I immediately stressed my disapproval. I had a feeling that this could only lead to problems in the future because of the personalities of everyone involved. My opinions and concerns were eventually thrown by the wayside and he was kept as a full-time Avon employee. "R" probably worked for us for over a year. During that time I heard many complaints that he stole overtime hours, would disappear during the day, would take forever to do a job, etc. Nobody ever said anything to him about this out of "respect" to me, but eventually he was fired by my uncles. Upon his firing, he typed a letter and hand delivered it to my parents' house. This letter would be the beginning of major problems for the families because the letter expressed that he was not going to pay for any part of the wedding and would not allow my uncles to attend the wedding. Lindsey's whole immediate family tried to turn Lindsey against me and split us up. Nonstop problems went on for over a year. Lin and I were put in the middle of things that were not our fault/problem. During this time, Lindsey asked me not to say anything to her family because it would start more problems. Things actually got to such a bad point that I talked Lin into totally changing our wedding plans and moving the date up so that we could just get it done as soon as possible.

Since the firing and until this moment, there has been a constant barrage of negative things said about me and my family by her family. I was always one of "them" and was thus tainted and a bad person. Their daughter "could do better". I hated them for what they had said about me and done to the two of us. The stuff that was said was never told directly to me, but rather to Lindsey, who would then relay it to me. This would infuriate me, but I was still not allowed to confront them. I would internalize all of this, bottle it up, and withdraw deeper into myself. I was often confronted by Lindsey to go out to dinner with them or go over their house. I would repeatedly say "no" due to my personal feelings about what they had done, but they would throw a considerable amount of guilt onto Lindsey. That guilt then turned into guilt onto me. I would suck up my pride and go. By being forced to go and to put on the "mask" pretending that everything was status quo, I fell deeper and deeper inside myself and inside my disorder. I would then restrict and hurt myself because, in my eyes, everybody was hurting me.

Things did not change once we got married. There still were negative things said about me, and done to us. I was labeled "tainted, sick, and defective" after it was revealed to them that I had an eating disorder. They never offered any support to me while I had my struggles. I was just the sick boy that was never going to be able to take care of their daughter.

There are so many other instances and examples (that I would love to include) at what horrible people they are and how they have been horrible to our relationship and to my personal well being, but I do not have the time and/or energy to go over them all. I do believe, however, that one incident should be mentioned because it is directly related to my recent collapse and subsequent hospitalization. When Lindsey got sick with vertigo, as was mentioned earlier, I had to pick up the slack, work more and bring home all the money for the household. As a result of this, her parents were asked to take her to different doctors and places for testing and other such things to see what was wrong with her and/or how to make her feel better. During these times, it was often directly stated by them that I was not able to provide for her and not able to be a husband to her. In their eyes, I was just a piece of shit and the only ones that could take care of Lindsey were her father, mother, and brother. Lindsey would not stand up to them for me when this happened, but rather would respond with a bitchy comment and change the subject. Once returning home from being with them however, the information was often relayed to me. Imagine how I felt when I came home each day after a long stressful nine hours at work to my wife and dog, not knowing if they were dying or not, and hearing all the things that were said about me. It hurt me and it hurt me very badly. I wanted to get on the phone and let them all know what I thought about what they had said, and tell them to "go fuck themselves". The problem however, was that I was never allowed to. Lindsey thought it would cause more problems and wanted me to basically suck it up and not do anything that would create any more harm to the situation. I was also forced to go over their house and see them. I put that fake smile on during dinner and played "happy", knowing that I truly hated them. I would be lying if I said that this did not hurt me. I felt like my wife was condoning the behaviors of her parents and maybe in the back of my mind I started to believe what they were

saying. She did not stand up to them. She did not tell
them to stop. She did not let me tell them what I
wanted... maybe they were telling the truth. It wasn't
the first time that people were saying these things about
me so I had a hard time disproving it. It hurt. It hurt
really badly, and it also crushed any bit of self-esteem
and self-worth that I had built up over the prior months.
Everything was happening all over again. People were
starting to say that I was useless and a bad person.
Nobody stood up for me and I couldn't stand up for
myself. There was only one way for me to cope with
all of this. I had my old friend tapping me on the
shoulder and whispering in my ear to remind me of this.
While this was all happening I began to see that this
situation with Lindsey's parents might lead me back
down the dark road that I had once traveled. I
remember two or three occasions where I literally
begged Lindsey to tell them off, stand up to them for
me, or let me stand up to them. I also begged not to be
forced into doing things with them. I told her that if
this did not happen then I would get sicker. That is

probably the thing that still hurts me the most. I basically told Lindsey, on my hands and knees and virtually in tears, that I was going to get sick again and she did nothing about it. She was the person that I loved and trusted more than anybody in this world and I felt like she did not care if I got sick again or not, and thus I took care of myself the only way that I truly knew how to.

It wasn't until after the Christmas holidays that Lindsey agreed with me, saw that her parents were a bunch of fucked up people. She saw how badly their words and actions affected me. She couldn't deny the impact on me anymore, especially since I was withdrawn from everybody, detached, and depressed to all hell on Christmas day. As everybody was celebrating the holiday and having a great time, I was in such a depressive state that I literally wanted to jump into the river behind my parents' house, sink to the bottom, and never come back. Lindsey cut most ties from her family, but didn't let them know this or why she had done so. The damage to me had been done and there really was nothing anybody could do to stop my decline.

The pressures at work kept building and building and I felt like I wasn't getting any help. I started eating less and less because that was the only thing I felt I could control in my life. I started sneaking exercise as I would do "random" sets of pushups at just about every second I had a free second to sneak away. I would do this under my desk or in the "plan" room at work, in the bathroom at home, in the basement, etc. I would run up and down stairs at the office and at home. If nobody was going to help me and was going to punish me in some way or another then I was going to cope with the feelings my way. I was truly returning to old form.

I was soon finding just about any way to restrict what I was eating and trying to work off what I had eaten in one way or another. I began using new tricks such as eating a lot of low calorie foods to make it appear as though I was eating a good amount of food. I became a "vegetarian", where I would give the appearance that I was eating normally but doing it in a restrictive way at the same time. Through my experience here at Princeton I have come to see that many of us here are "vegetarians". I can easily say that I was not doing it for any reason other than to further my eating disorder and destroy myself. I returned to the old habit of eating virtually the same things everyday. I pushed my meal times back later and later each night so as to delay the process of eating as long as I could. I began using my food rituals again. I felt my clothes getting looser and looser again and became paranoid if I felt a little bloated and/or stuffed because it made me feel fat. I occasionally got on the scale to see how low I had gotten, and would get upset if I was not as low as I would have liked. I would then try doing behaviors that would help me get to the low weight that I wanted. I became obsessed with seeing every bone in my body. If I could not count every rib through my torso and through my back then I was not pleased. The funny part is that I never set or wanted a specific weight. It was more like I just wanted to see how low I really could go. My goal was to physically get as far away from the 290lb person that existed years ago, and still existed in my head.

I also began taking advantage of the fact that my body would sometimes make me burp food up into my mouth after I had eaten it. This was probably due to my body not being used to having certain kinds of food in it. I never forced myself to get sick or anything like that, but if my body shot food back up into my throat or mouth, I would spit it out. I would do this in parking lots of restaurants, out of car windows, at home, in the garbage at work, etc. It was a side effect of not eating. I was happy to use it to my advantage. I was also becoming creative and trying out new tricks to restrict. Since people were watching me with an incredible hawk eye, I had to find secretive ways to avoid consuming the food. I began holding food in my mouth and then find a way to spit it out. I would go into the bathroom and spit it out, or spit it in to my napkin at the table. While out at dinner I would just flat out throw food on the floor when nobody was looking. In addition to that, I also began dumping food down the drain or throwing it in the garbage whenever the opportunity arose. I would wait until Lindsey went into the shower in the morning to dump my nutrition shake down the kitchen drain or cook something in the microwave and quickly throw it in the garbage can outside so that the smell lingered in the kitchen. I was pulling out all stops to make my disorder happy, and it was pulling out all stops to kill me.

Mentally, I was exhausted and miserable. I was diving into work, and the pressure was giving my disorder all the fuel that it needed to run my life. I would get to work at least a half an hour early and refuse to leave work earlier than 5 o'clock in the afternoon. I would occasionally stay late. I would sink into deep depressions at work again. I listened to a particular radio show that played all day long, which talked regularly about people's bodies, what foods are bad, and other such issues. I didn't know it then, but this particular program triggered my disorder into hyper drive and made me further restrict certain types of food.

Other than that, I knew what I was doing and knew that my disorder had full control over me again. I really did nothing to try to fix it. It was something familiar to me in a world full of chaos. I was so mentally worn out from everything that I just gave up trying to fight it. I did things like reading or watching movies to just take my mind off the thoughts and delay any type of exercise or meal times. I often considered my disorder my best friend. It is there all the time, will not hurt me, will not betray or leave me, is there to protect me from others, and basically is my safety net. All of this is not true, of course, but that is what it feels like once the monster has its grip onto you. It gives you a false sense of control and protection that is so hard to discard. I once again returned into that "dark" place where I had no ambition to do anything and no drive to have fun. I lost that little bit of smile that I had earned back over the months and I had no motivation. I had no desires. I basically had no life. My father asked me, before I became hospitalized, what my dreams and hopes were. The answer was simply this: "I have no dreams. I do not look to the future, and I do not have any hopes". It is a sad thing to realize, but it was exactly the way I was feeling at the time. I lost all ability to look at the future or look forward to things in life. There was "nothing" good in my life that I could see which was worth looking forward to. I was not looking forward to children. I was not looking forward to a long life with Lindsey. I was not looking forward to life at all. The only thing that I would think about was how was I going to get through another day living like this, and if I get through today, then how was I going to try to get through tomorrow. I did not care. I was…basically giving up again.

And give up is what I did. I lost my drive to get better and gave in to all of the thoughts that were going through my head. I let the monster control me once again and I didn't care if I hurt myself or anybody else in the process. My wife, mom, dad, brother, uncles, co-workers, etc. all tried to talk to me about my situation and tried to influence me to get better. Some would plead and cry, some would yell and scream, and some would talk sternly and authoritatively. They all had their ways, and they all tried, but I did not listen. I really did not give a shit. They wanted me to go see a therapist again, whether it be Dr. E. or someone else, but I could not allow myself to do this again. When I started seeing Dr. E. initially I formed a good rapport with the man. He did shed some light on my situation and unlock many of the emotions that I had locked away for so long. He unlocked them but he never taught me how to cope with them. I was all of a sudden exposed to some really powerful feelings and emotions and had no way of coping with them. I was not "allowed" to use all the behaviors I had previously used, but was given no direction with any new methods to use in order to cope. I was able to work through the time I was seeing him without these coping skills but once everything started falling around me and I began to relapse, the only things I knew how to use were my disordered behaviors. More importantly, the reason I would not allow myself to see anybody again was the fact that I felt extremely betrayed by Dr. E. As I stated earlier, he and I reached a point where he cut me loose and said he would call me in two weeks to check on me and see if I wanted to set up another appointment. Well those two weeks passed and then two more and then two more. I never heard from him again. I started resenting him for this. I truly trusted and opened up to this man and thought that we had formed somewhat of a therapeutic "friendship". I thought he cared about me and about my well-being. After not hearing from him again, I felt that I was nothing but another case file in his cabinet. I began to see myself not as a person that he cared about but rather nothing more than a person who writes him a check every week. He was the first person that I allowed inside my head and this is how he repaid me. From that moment on, I was very resentful and had no trust in therapists or in treatment all together.

I was not going to change, and that was that. This was my life and I was "happy" with it. Truth be told, I was not happy at all, but rather very much afraid of giving up my best friend. By giving it up I would have to totally change myself. This disorder has been everything to me since 2002. It has been involved in every action, thought, and spoken word from the second I woke up to the second I went to bed each day of each year. It was everything that I knew and I did not know/remember life without it. It was my identity, the way I felt special, and it made me who I thought I wanted to be. The thought of giving all of this up and completely changing really scared the hell out of me, and made me not want to change even more. I faded away both physically and mentally/emotionally. I was deeply depressed and inverted more than any other time in the past. My body became more emaciated than ever. My blood pressure and pulse plummeted once again and I had the dizzy spells as well. In earlier stages of my disorder I grew cold easily, but now I seemed to be cold all the time. I was cold from the second I woke up to the second I went to sleep and would not get any warmer when I would dress in layers. I would have to clothe myself in layers and layers of sweatshirts, sweaters, etc. I would turn on the gas burners on the stove to warm my hands, and turn the heat on during the summer time. It seemed that there was nothing I could do to make the coldness go away. My hands and feet were always white. They hurt from the cold and would never get warm. I got to such a bad point physically that Lindsey would wake up several times a night and make sure that I was still breathing. It was a very scary time for her.

I was reaching the point where mentally I felt like I was ready to give up on life again and I physically felt like I was headed in the direction of death. There just was no physical way that I could have kept going the way I was. Through his tirades, rants, and screams at me, my brother had said numerous times that I probably needed to "go away" because it was obvious that I could not control this monster on my own. He was exactly right that I could not control it, but of course I denied this and did not want to hear anything of the sort. But after hearing this many times and by many different people, including Lindsey, I started to give it some thought. I was at the point where work at

Avon Contractors had beaten me into a lump of shit and worn me down to such a point where I was totally exhausted and utterly useless. I could not think. I could not concentrate on anything but my disorder. My disorder had one goal this time, and that was to kill me. I was going along with it without a problem. My dad forced me to take a week off and it was on that week off that I made a pretty big decision. On the first Monday of March 2008, I had a conversation with my sister regarding the possibility of going to the hospital. I asked if she would tell everyone for me, if I decided to do so. She agreed that rehab was the best option and that she would tell everyone my decision. I really had no life at this point, there was no ambition, there was no joy, there was no peace, and there was no light in my eyes. I was so depressed that I really knew I could not go on with this. Either I was going to kill it or it was going to kill me. So after some self-thought and debate I decided to throw in the towel and ask for some real help to try to beat this thing. I decided this on that first Monday but was not going to say anything until that

Friday. I did not want anything to interfere with my brother's birthday. We waited and then Jessica told everyone for me. I could not be there or tell anyone because I was too ashamed of myself, feeling I was too weak to beat this monster on my own. They eventually made me come over to the house and we all had a very emotional conversation. Lindsey was yelling at me, my dad was yelling at me, my mom and brother were both upset, and I as usual was totally blank, stone faced, and unaffected by what they were saying to me. Eventually I told them everything and then started to cry hysterically. All of the emotions that I had bottled up had suddenly come bursting out. I told them how I felt. I said that I was too ashamed to tell them, and that I was ready to give it all up and start life. I felt tired of living this way. We researched a few places and made a few phone calls but I would have to wait until Monday morning until I would be able to talk to anybody. It was a very emotional weekend to say the least. Lindsey and I were very upset because we knew that we would have to be apart from each other for a period of time.

We stayed up most of that night just holding each other because we were both very afraid. Separately, I was extremely emotional because I knew that what I was going to have to do was going to be extremely hard.

Monday morning came and we got the woman from the treatment center on the phone. I answered a ton of questions that she asked me. I tried to tell her how urgent it was that I got into their program because I knew deep down inside that if I didn't get in then I would eventually be dead. This was going to be my last shot at it. I did everything that I needed to do to get an interview at the program, including rushing to my primary doctor's office to get weighed and have him write that it was necessary for me to receive hospitalization. When all was said and done I had to go to the hospital the next day, Tuesday, for an evaluation with the doctor. I had to pack/bring all my stuff in case I got admitted. Tuesday morning came and the ride to University Medical Center at Princeton was a long one, full of different emotions for me. I was scared, angry, nervous, anxious, relieved, etc. all at the same time.

We got to the hospital, filled out tons of paperwork, answered questions from different people, had a consultation with Dr. W (the founder of the program), and was ultimately admitted into the inpatient program. As Dr. W interviewed me it became very apparent to him that I needed help and that I needed help fast. He made me get on the scale and the result was quite shocking. I was at my all time lowest weight at 134lbs (over 10lbs lighter than when I was seeing Dr. E). I weighed less than many women in my life and really was knocking at death's door. When taking a tour of the place and seeing the other patients I quickly compared myself to them and said that I was not as sick as them and that I did not belong there. I was still in some sort of denial all the way up until the last second. Maybe I really didn't need to be there. I remember being so extremely upset and scared when I was going through the motions of checking in, having my baggage searched, being told all the rules, and being watched as I ate my first meal. Then it finally hit me: "Holy Shit, this is for real!" I watched as Lindsey, Mom, and Dad walked out, and the doors closed. Then I turned around and walked toward what I hope would be a new life.

As soon as they left I was thrown into my first group, and I made the decision to quickly open up and start talking. I figured that since I'm here I better take full advantage of it. I felt like I was bounced around all over the place, meeting all these staff people, and most importantly meeting people that were like me. Soon after my admittance, Dr. W had to give me a physical examination and he pointed something out to me that I could not deny, no matter how hard my eating disorder tried to blind me. I mentioned to him that I was cold all of the time and he then made me look at my fingernails. At first I did not notice anything different or unusual about them, but when he laid his hand against mine I noticed that my fingertips were blue. My body was keeping the blood flow close to my heart and organs and restricting the amount of blood that was going to my extremities. Seeing my body turn a color it should not have been, gave me a slap in the face and forced any bit of denial I may have had right out of me. As I went into my second group someone asked me the dumbest question I think I've ever been asked in my life. Darlene, one of the nutritional counselors asked me "What do you want to eat for dinner?" I remember basically finding a good way to say, "Go fuck yourself" and had her pick out something for me and do my menu for the next day. I was so shell-shocked that first day, I basically walked around like a deer in headlights. When all was said and done, after that first day, mixed in with the emotions of fear, anxiety, and exhaustion, was the very obvious feeling that a huge weight was lifted off of my shoulders. Behind it all was a sense of hope and peace that had not been there before. I remember thinking that, at least for now, I did not have to worry about anything else but me. I embraced the possibility that maybe all the torment I was going through would end. As long as I was in this place it seemed that there was going to be no more hiding my behaviors, no more lying to my loved ones, no secrets kept, and most importantly there wouldn't be any shame or embarrassment about what I was dealing with.

I slept better that night than any other night since my disorder began.

This all leads me to today. The inpatient program here is making me tap into and face emotions that I have avoided and locked away for so long. There are very strict rules, some of which make no sense, and are quite humiliating for a person my age but they are there for a reason. It is very humbling when you cannot go to the bathroom without telling a nurse and when you have to strip naked, put on a small gown, and get weighed at 6am every morning. They monitor everything about you. They record the amount of water you drink, the amount of walking around you do, the amount of socializing you do. I am not complaining about the rules one bit because I know that they are put in place by very smart people that have been dealing with eating disorders for a very long time. But I feel sometimes that there is no difference in the rules between 12 year-olds and 25 year-olds. You are very restricted with what you can do. This is absolutely wonderful because they force me to use methods of coping with things other than the eating disorder behaviors that I was so accustomed to using. I am in here with a great bunch of patients and for the first time I have been able to see anorexia and bulimia. I am surrounded by BOTH men and women of all ages (11-33 years of age) that are dealing in one way or another with the exact same thing that I am. I can physically see what anorexia can do to a body. I can actually see it in other people, and it is very scary to say the least. I can see the same blank stare in their eyes. I can see the panic when mealtime comes, and I can see the struggle they have dealing with something that is controlling them. But above anything else I am able to see through the eating disorder in each person and see really beautiful people. I see all of these beautiful people that think of themselves as shit and don't care if they wither away and totally destroy themselves. They are absolutely the greatest people I have ever met in my life. I want each of them to get through their ordeal. There are a certain few people that I have become close with and am figuratively walking hand-in-hand with through the journey of recovery. We are here. We all pick each other up when are down. We talk and vent to each other. We connect with each other more than anybody else in our lives. We are sharing something that nobody else can share with us. It is the first time in a very long time that I do not feel like I am different and stand out in one way or another. I have felt for a very long time that I am either standing alone in a very big, dark room or that I am standing all alone in a very crowded room. I do not feel any of this here. I feel like I can be "me" and nobody will judge me. It is so difficult to see why each of them does what they do to themselves, and how each views himself or herself. I must constantly remind myself that I act in similar ways towards myself. I cannot separate myself from them. I cannot fool myself or blind myself by how I am mentally and physically destroying myself. It makes me think that since I see these people as being beautiful and amazing people then maybe they see me as the same and maybe I am not as bad as I thought I was for so long.

I am feeling a whirlwind of emotions right now.
I have really tapped into things that I have locked away
for years. It is not like it was when I was seeing Dr. E.
once every week for an hour. No, now I meet with my
therapist every day for one hour, my psychiatrist for
half an hour or so, have 3-4 groups per day, and have to
be re-fed. Dr. W took my case on personally and as my
psychiatrist he monitors and controls everything about
my treatment. He is a great and very intelligent man.
My therapist's name is Amy. Once I found out her
name was Amy I had concerns due to my dealings in
the past with other women named Amy. But I made a
decision to break down the barriers and open up to her.
I hope I have a chance to write more about her in the
future because so far my relationship with Amy has
been extremely beneficial. She is allowing me to open
up with her, and walking me through this with her hand
on my shoulder. She shows compassion, which is
something I have not received before. Apart from the
one-on-one therapy, I also have many groups per day. I
have group psychotherapy, Connections group, Coping

Skills group, Nutrition group, Goals group, Art Therapy group, Yoga group, Weekend Processing group, etc. Even though many groups might seem "stupid" to me at times I am trying to approach each with an open mind and really use each group to my advantage.

My nutritionist, Kristen, is in charge of my re-feeding. The re-feeding process is a nightmare to say the least. I am ingesting way more calories than I have in a long time and am being forced to eat all of those foods that I labeled "bad" for so long. Along with forcing me to take in my calories I am inundated with factual information regarding what a body needs to function, what the purpose of carbohydrates/fat/protein is in the body, and the truth about what happens to the body as it is being starved. Yes, I am admitting that I was starving myself to death. We watched a video based on an experiment done just after World War II regarding the effects of starvation on the body and how to re-feed it properly. The participants who volunteered for the study went through a period of partial starvation and rigorous exercise to see the effects on the body. As

I was watching this, I saw major similarities between what they were experiencing and what I used to experience. They were physically exhausted, could not think or focus, were depressed all of the time, had no sexual desires, etc. I was astonished because I saw myself in each of these men, and was hit hard by the realization that I really was starving myself. There was no way I could ever deny it now. Unfortunately, during the re-feeding process your body goes into a hyper-metabolic state because it was deprived for so long and it takes eating a considerable amount of calories for weight gain to happen. My calories had to keep going up and up. I walk around here being completely stuffed and quite disgusted with my body. It seems like every other day I am getting another calorie increase. As one would expect, this brings out a great deal of emotions because for so long I have connected food and my body with emotions. There have been times when I have just wanted to curl into a ball and scream as loud as I can or cry my eyes out. I hate the way I feel. I want to turn around and run full speed back to my "friend" but I know I cannot. I will not survive it this time if I do.

The amount of therapy (psychological and nutritional) is quite overwhelming thus far and I have gone through times where I questioned whether I really want to go through this and give up my disorder. I have felt extremely conflicted at times as my disorder is screaming and trying to grab onto any little thing it can to lure me back. It is in panic mode and it is pulling out all stops to keep me. As I stated earlier, my eating disorder was all that I had for 6 years. It was involved with every action, emotion, thought, etc. It was my best friend and my worst enemy, but above all it was something familiar and "comfortable". There is a lyric in the song "Landslide" by Fleetwood Mack that goes: "I've been afraid of changing because I've built my life around you." I remember listening to this song during one of the groups and it struck a chord with how I felt then and how I am feeling now. I have built everything around this. I am scared out of my mind about the concept of changing. I am afraid to take that risk and see what life is like without my disorder. In a way, I feel as though my disorder made me special. I am very afraid of the unknown, but I know that I should at least take a peek over the mountain to see what life is like. I do know that if I do not like what this new life has to offer I can just run right back, but it is getting to the point where I want to take that peek. On top of it all, I am very anxious, extremely emotional, and disgusted with the way I feel. This is the exact type of situation that my eating disorder thrived on in the past. At times it seemed to have been winning as I would hide some exercise here and there, but I have made the conscious decision that if I chose to go through with this process then I am going to do it 100% with no turning back. It will be a difficult decision to say the least. I have so much more to do here at Princeton and so much more work to do when I eventually get out. This is the hardest thing I have ever done, and I do not know if I can keep going. Do I really want this or will I just play the game for now and then return to my normal behaviors once I get out of here? Is it really worth it? I have to keep reassuring myself that this is what my disorder wants. It wants me to question everything. It wants me to hold on. It wants to keep control of me, and it eventually wants to kill me.

One thing that I have realized here in treatment is that I want to live. I have been physically alive for the past 6 years but have not been "alive". My eating disorder took everything out of my life and the only things it gave me were pain and suffering. I have lost the ability to smile, to laugh, to have fun, and to enjoy the simple things. As I sit here I realize that I have seen glimpses of the good that can come with being freed from the chains of this disorder, and I do want the ability to smile, laugh, have fun, and enjoy the simple things. I don't want to worry what people say to me or what food will be present at a meal. I have a picture of Lindsey and I hanging on my bulletin board with the words "My Reason" scribbled above. The picture serves as my motivation to get through this. I want to get healthy for her, for us. I want to be able to grow old with Lindsey and have children and be happy together.

I want to be able to show love and receive love. I want to be able to love Victor Camillo Avon, IV. You know, something must be headed in the right direction because the last few sentences were focused on what I want and not what everybody else wants. I am doing this for me and I only hope that I am really seeing the light at the end of this really long and dark tunnel.

Conclusion

This final installment of my story is being written six months after I was officially discharged from Princeton University Medical Center and have had the opportunity to experience the journey of recovery in the "real world". The last time I stroked the keys of this keyboard I was very conflicted about whether or not I wanted to really let go of my disorder and start life anew. I laid in bed one night shortly after our 9 o'clock snack time and made a commitment to the picture of Lindsey and I on my bulletin board that I would give my all to fight this, and truly change. It was the hardest decision I have ever had to make. I knew what I was going to have to do and I would not let anything get in my way.

I do not want it to sound like I made this decision all by myself and that all was "hunky-dory" afterwards. The one person that was most instrumental in leading me to that decision and to the point where I am today was my therapist Amy. Amy was my angel. I'm not sure if I can clearly articulate all the emotions

and thoughts I have regarding her and what she has
helped me through, but I will give it my best shot
because I feel that she deserves it. I was very fortunate
to have Amy take my case on. I was her last official
case because she was eight months pregnant. I was not
sure if I could open up to another therapist after feeling
such a betrayal of my trust by Dr. E, but I quickly
sensed that the two therapists were not in the same
ballpark. I noticed Amy had a real sense of compassion
for what I had been through. It seemed like she actually
cared about ME and MY feelings. Earlier I made a
reference to Dante and how he got out of hell, but I
failed to mention that in that story Dante makes it out
only due to the guidance provided by Virgil. Virgil
pushed Dante along when he was scared and when he
did not want to go anymore. Amy was my Virgil. She
was the force that kept pushing me forward when I was
too scared to go by myself. She was the comforting
hand on my shoulder telling me everything was going
to be all right. She was right there for me every step of
the way, not letting me turn back, and convincing me it

will be okay if I keep going forward. She was the first person to ever tell me it was okay to have a bad day, and wanted to talk about why it was a bad day. She made me do exercises to recognize what I got from my disorder and what the disorder has taken from me. Amy brought thoughts and feelings out of me that I had locked away for so long. I relived everything from my childhood, being overweight, the move to Wall Township, betrayals, the issues at work, the issues with Lindsey's and my parents. She made me experience all of those emotions again, but was right there to help me get through them. She even forced me to have a meeting with Lindsey and both of her parents where I expressed my feelings and discussed how I perceived things. I was not surprised that they saw nothing wrong with anything that they did. But the best thing that came out of the whole ordeal was that Lindsey got a chance to see the people that they really were for the first time. The All-American façade was dropped. Their claws came out for a fight as they defended how they acted. They began putting blame on me and

Lindsey for how we felt. The meeting lasted about two hours and I was emotionally exhausted afterwards. That was the last time I saw either of them and even though nothing was resolved I feel as though I was vindicated for feeling the way that I did. There was closure for me in the sense that they knew I did not want to and could not have a relationship with them. I got through this session only because I had my protector, my Virgil, sitting right beside me and pushing me along.

Unfortunately, Amy left to go on maternity leave just prior to my discharge to the outpatient program. She made sure things were in order for me before she left. She set me up with her replacement in Princeton, Margo. She also helped me through everything. Amy was the stern, yet compassionate kick in the ass that I needed as an inpatient, while Margo was the passive, sweet, and knowledgeable guide that I needed through my outpatient treatment. Amy was my Yin and Margo was the Yang that formed the total package to get me to the place I am now. After Amy left, I was not only mourning the loss of my disorder, but also really started to mourn the loss of her. The relationship that Amy and I developed was the one thing that I needed most in my time of need. She was more than a therapist. She was my friend. I can say without a shadow of a doubt that Amy saved my life and I will never forget her for as long as I live.

As time passed by, I began noticing that my fellow patients started turning to me for advice or looked to me for some inspiration. I was repeatedly told that I was the reason that certain people continued to try to break their personal curse. I took on the mentor role, and became like a big brother to the young men and women that I had the privilege of meeting on the unit. I truly wanted each and every person to succeed and would do anything to help them get through their recovery. I knew what each of them was feeling because I too had the calorie increases, the horrible body image, the extreme mental anguish, the family problems, etc. and would sit by them for support or talk things out with them. I told stories of all the bad things that could come from having an eating disorder. I repeatedly begged them to seriously try to part with their disorder while they were young so that they would not have to endure what I had. The very last group of my final day at the hospital was dedicated to me and each patient made cards for me to take on my journey. I was extremely touched by each and every one of them, and still read them as a form of motivation and a reminder that there are people out there that really care about the real me. I will never forget the young men and women I met on the unit. I wish each of them the absolute best in their recoveries, and hope that they can each find the strength to live happy, healthy, eating disorder-free lives.

Everyone looked up to me and came to me for inspiration, but recovery was not a walk in the park for me. My hospitalization was the hardest thing I have ever done. Even up until my last day there, I had days and nights where I wanted to scream. I remember crying a few times while lying in bed at home because of how I felt inside my body. I literally curled up into a ball in the corner of the room because of what I was physically becoming, what I was mentally experiencing, and the fear I was feeling. I was forcing myself to do what I was most scared of in life. I was forcing myself to gain weight again, and I was forcing myself to experience things that I locked up for so long. My greatest fear in the world then and now is that I will return to the point physically and experience all the things I did so many years before when I was heavy. It was so hard trusting what everybody was telling me, and it was considerably hard to trust myself and my body. The hardest part of it all was the fact that I knew going back was not an option. I could not let myself down. I couldn't let Lindsey down. I truly felt like I could not let my fellow patients down. I began to really see the light for the first time in my life, but those dark shadows were continually trying to black it all out. Everyday was an uphill battle but I would not let myself fall back down when I had worked so hard to get that far up.

When I was officially discharged from
Princeton I had this feeling of invincibility, and a
completely different outlook on life. I was happy about
everything. I was happy the birds were flying. I was
happy the trees were green. I was happy to be alive,
and I was happy that I could conquer to world.
Unfortunately this honeymoon period did not last
forever as the real world really does not care that people
are in recovery. People say triggering things all of the
time without even realizing it. I realize I am
"environmentally" triggered. I had a hard time
returning to places such as my house and work. These
were places that I would sit and suffer in silence and
just being back in certain rooms and seats brought back
all of the memories and emotions. It took a very long
time to get used to creating new memories in these
places. Obviously, going to the food store for the first
time was incredibly hard and continues to be a
challenge from time to time. Going out to restaurants is
also difficult. Probably the most frustrating thing is that
family members seem to forget certain things they

learned in the hospital. People have gone back to using old behaviors. Information learned during therapy seems to have gone in one ear and out the other. It seems like everyone in my life feels that I am "cured" as if I had a cold that went away. Because I am not physically at the point I was when I was really in my disorder, the majority of people think everything is normal with me. They view me as being fine. They think that I can do anything, talk about anything, and eat anything. They do not keep in mind that everyday is a battle I fight. It is a very frustrating feeling, and I have felt many times that people simply do not care about what I am going through. Lindsey has been the only one to truly stay mindful and have an open mind about everything. She has truly been my shoulder to lean on and has given me strength when I needed it.

Before Amy left Princeton on maternity leave, she made sure I had an outside treatment team set up for me once I was discharged. She set me up with Dr. Marnie Fegan as my psychologist and Donna Gallagher as my dietician/nutritionist. I was a little apprehensive about opening myself up to more people but I had to trust Amy's decision. I can easily say that meeting Marnie and Donna has been the best thing that could have happened to me. They are very intelligent, caring, thoughtful, and overall great people to be around. Both have helped me get through so much and I can say that I don't know if I could have gotten through so much outside of the hospital without their help. They provide me with the necessary counseling and guidance to get over each and every hurdle or struggle that comes my way. They are not my "therapists" as Dr. E. was, they are my friends and they are one more blessing that Amy has provided to me.

Marnie and Donna host a support group that happens every first and third Thursday of the month. I attend the group religiously as it is the only time when I truly feel safe and comfortable to be myself. Even though we see each other only 2 times a month, the people that attend this group have formed such a close bond that we each truly care about one another. Each of us is at a different point in our own recovery but we all have a common bond that not many people can share. I am so glad that I have them all in my life because most of the time I still feel like I am alone in this world, mainly because I go through something each and every day that the greater majority of people can not comprehend. That is one of the more difficult things I have learned about recovery. It is hard going through life with almost 100% of the people around me either having no concept of an eating disorder, or uneducated on the subject. Some don't even care about it all together. It is a very lonely feeling and I still feel like I am all alone in that crowded room from time to time. When I am around the people in the group I feel as though I am among people that "get" what I go through, will never judge me, and will accept me for who I am.

I am forever grateful for this new group of "extended family", but I truly cherish the relationship I still have with some of my fellow inpatients. Several of us keep in close contact as we are constantly text messaging or emailing one another. We are there to share in each other's achievements and we are there to support one another when we are struggling. I do love each of them and hope we stay in touch with each other for a very long time.

When all was said and done, I was smacked in the face by the realization that it is not "game over" for my eating disorder, but rather I have reached level two with a long battle in front of me. That pink cloud I was on and the feeling that I had truly conquered something, went away and I was left with the fact that I will have to keep fighting my monster for probably the rest of my life. It has been a hard realization to accept. I have had to ask myself over and over again if it really was worth it to keep fighting. My disorder has tried to challenge my strength and take over again. It has thrown roadblocks in front of me that I thought I could not pass. It has amplified every negative body feeling I have. It has tormented me with every negative thought it could throw at me. It has pestered me over and over and over again. It felt like my disorder was in the backseat as I was driving a car and it kept nagging me to turn around, just waiting until I got tired and just listened to it to shut it up. It has shown me every "good" thing that it ever provided me and tried to lure me back. Sure, it did provide me with good things, but for some reason it is only the good things that are easily remembered. It seems as though I have disregarded all of the negative things that my disorder provided me. I need to keep reminding myself everyday. I am reminded everyday when my legs, knees, hips, and shoulder ache due to the exercise I put myself through. I have to live with the regret that I pushed away the majority of people I had in my life. I have to live with the fact that I know I intentionally hurt Lindsey and my family members. I have to live with the fact that I did not go out and do things that normal people in their early twenties do. I have to live with the fact that I had no urge to have fun, and hated life. I have to live with the fact that there was not one day that I could "turn it off". I couldn't shut it off for birthdays, parties, or even my wedding and I have to live with the fact that I could not even push myself to eat my own wedding cake. I have had days and weeks where I have struggled but I have never EVER used my behaviors to cope with what I was feeling. My eating disorder has used every technique possible to get me to turn back but I refuse to give it that power anymore. I gave it so much power and control for so long that I cannot let it take anything else from me. I will never feel as bad in my recovery as I did in my disorder. To steal a line from Donna it is absolutely true that "your worst day in recovery is better than your best day in your disorder".

Turning back would be the easy thing to do. It would all just be so simple if I threw in the towel, refused to fight any more, gave in, and ultimately perished. But that is what my disorder wants me to think. The hard option is choosing to fight this and keep going straight on the road to recovery. I am driven in hope of one day reaching that pink cloud that I had when I left the hospital. I truly saw how wonderful life can be and how peaceful I could live without my little "friend" whispering in my ear 24 hours a day. Plus, through the help of Lindsey, Amy,

Donna, Marnie, and the rest of my new family I have grown to learn that there are people that really truly care about me for who I am. They have allowed me to see that I am genuinely a good person and people want to know and be friends with me. Yes, there are many times that I feel like that fat little kid standing in front of the room in his underwear, but there are many more times where I feel more confident about myself and about my ability to live my life.

Recovery is the hardest thing anybody can go through. I hope by reading this you can take something positive away from my story. I literally walked through hell for all of those years, but in the end I am more focused on recovering than ever before. I am not "cured" by any means but I know that where I am is a hell of a lot better than where I was. It is an everyday struggle but I want you to know that it is a struggle that is well worth it. The book I read regarding anorexia, specifically male anorexia, was not a positive one in the slightest and it did not paint a good picture of recovery or treatment. I can seriously say that devoting myself to treatment and choosing recovery saved my life. It is incredibly sad to watch the people that I have grown close to as they struggle with their own personal monster and sometimes give into it, but the one thing I try to hammer into their heads is that recovery can work as long as you are willing to do whatever it takes to achieve it. As I conclude this book, journal, or whatever it is called I would like to leave you with one final story. When I left the hospital I immediately tattooed the words "Stronger Than Death" on the left side on my stomach signifying that I am stronger than any eating disorder. A week later I tattooed a phrase that was given to me upon my discharge by a good friend of mine. It is across my rib cage and stomach and it serves as a motivator every day when I look at myself. It sums up the journey that is my recovery and helps me when I am struggling. It reads: "Courage does not roar…It is the quiet voice at the end of the day that whispers… I will begin again tomorrow".

There are times when I want to go running back to my monster. There are times when it seems the fight is too much. There are times when I feel broken down. There are times when I want to curl up into a ball and cry. There are times when I get frustrated and tired of fighting. Regardless of it all, I know what I have to do and I know I am strong enough to overcome anything. I'm too stubborn of a son of a bitch to let it take me down again, and just like my stomach says: "I will begin again tomorrow".

Dedication

I am the first person to admit that I would not be here writing this today without the help, support, and love of certain people in my life. First, I have to thank my wife Lindsey for sticking with me through all the hard times. I have put you through things that you never should have been put through, and I hope I can make it up to you. I do not know why you stayed with me, but I am forever thankful that you did. Thank you for all of the love and support you have given me. I have to thank my father, mother, brother, sister, Nana, and Pops for being so persistent in your efforts to initiate the change in me. Your techniques may not have been the best but I always knew you cared about me. I will always know that my family did not give up on me when I gave up on myself.

I must dedicate this book to my fabulous treatment teams in Princeton and in Red Bank. Amy, you are my guardian angel. I cannot ever thank you enough for being the amazing person that you are. I credit so much to you, and will forever be thankful that you entered my life. You can deny it and place responsibility elsewhere, but I will always say that I left Princeton the way I did because of YOU. Dr. W, I will forever remember coming to you a broken "boy" and leaving a strong man. Accepting me into the program on that March morning was the greatest thing you could have done for me. You were my mentor, my advisor, and the person I trusted behind the wheel driving me towards a better life. I really think I would not be here today without your help. Thank you for everything you did and for every opportunity you gave me. Donna and Marnie, the two of you have been such huge parts of my life. Things have not been easy and everything that could challenge me seemed to have challenged me, and the both of you have helped me through it all. I don't know if I could have made it through all of the hard times without the D.G. and the C.C. The two of you have been more than a treatment team to me. You have been friends, and I am very blessed to have found you. I am a better person for having met the two of you. I must thank and dedicate this to Margo, Kristen, Audra,

Susan, Darlene, Kate, Kelly St., Kelly Sw, Beth, Janet, MJ, Kaelin, all the nurses, and the rest of the staff at the Princeton EDU. You were all a huge part of my recovery and helped guide me on my path to discharge and further. Each of you has left an everlasting mark on me and I can only wish I have done the same to you.

I have met dozens of wonderful people that suffer through this illness over the past year and a half, and each of them has touched me in one way or another. I thank you all for supporting me and allowing me to be "me". I want to dedicate this book every single one of them, and would like to send a special dedication to: Jeanine (my Princeton partner), Kim, Danielle, Jigga Jess, Jess M., Terri, Brittni, Pessie, Joel, Julia, Maureen, Laura, Natalie, Elliot, Kirsty, Bridget, Annie, Kelli, Rachel, Maddie, Sara, and Jen. I want to thank you all for accepting me and allowing me to be a part of your lives. My life is so much better now that I have had the chance to meet each of you.

Last, but not least, I would like to dedicate this book to anybody that is suffering through this disease, whether openly and in secret. You are not alone, and I hope you find the strength to overcome your personal monster. It's never too later to start your life over. Recovery is possible!

A very special dedication goes out to Donna Gallagher for helping this book become a reality. You put the air in my sails, steered me in the right directions, and made me feel passionate/proud of something for the first time in a very long time. I could not have done this without the love you have shown me.

Contribution by Donna Gallagher

Every once in a while a patient walks through the doors of our recovery center and I get a good feeling about them immediately, a good "recovery feeling". That is the feeling I had when Vic walked in. He appeared like a "man on a mission". His mission was to never let his eating disorder control his life, ever again. That meeting took place 2 years ago and he has never looked back!

Vic has unwaveringly made his recovery the top priority in his life. He is a self-described "tough son of a bitch". He has to be tough because he has an illness that is severe, complicated, and will take his life if he gives into it. His story is gripping. His recovery has been tough. And, because he is a male suffering from a traditionally female disease, his honesty is unexpected yet inspirational.

I have had the privilege of being Vic's nutrition therapist for 2 years. I am grateful for his trust and I am honored to be a part of his recovery journey.

I often say I wish all eating disorder sufferers could be like Vic. He has strength, perseverance, humor, and hope. These are some of the qualities that are vitally important in the recovery process. Hopefully, when people read his book, they will be inspired and find hope for themselves.

Recovery IS possible!

<u>Contribution by Dr. Marnie Fegan</u>

Eating disorders are inherently complex illnesses that are destructive in nature and often very difficult to overcome. I am fortunate to work with individuals in recovery; their perseverance is a constant source of inspiration. I am grateful for the opportunity to work with these strong individuals, some of who are the most remarkable people I have ever known.

I have had the privileged of treating Vic Avon for the past two years. His discharge from an intense, yet crucial inpatient stay serves as the starting point for our therapeutic journey. It was clear at our initial meeting that Vic was determined to keep his recovery on track and that any possibility of yielding to his illness was banished. It became very clear that Vic possessed the distinctive quality of 'infectious perseverance'. Not only did this help him fight through his illness but it created hope, inspiration and determination in others.

Vic's perseverance is illustrated in the intense account of his battle with Anorexia Nervosa. In his book, he describes so precisely the conditions of his illness and shares so honestly his struggles with an illness that is often mislabeled as "female". Vic's story is a wonderful tool not only for those in recovery, but for all individuals who have felt hopeless and immobilized by their struggles. His story is one that teaches how strength, courage, determination and faith can overcome hardships in a one's life. Although most will not have the opportunity to meet Vic, the hope and inspiration that is experienced when reading his book, is as if you did.

The Release

Words have built me,

Constructed from years of profanity,

There is no hope now,

Living a life of obscurity.

Seven years in the past,

Forming such a heavy load,

Your time has come,

Now you watch me explode.

Relentless abuse,

Constant pain,

Its makes me strong,

Allowing me to maintain.

Ring the bell,

All who dare,

Solitarily standing there,

No way to prepare.

The signs should have been read,

My Monster Within

Warning all to beware,

What waits inside,

None can compare.

Now you're frightened,

Can't help but stare,

Welcome motherfucker,

Now see the world that is my nightmare.

Nothings can stop it now,

No thought, no prayer,

You've pierced me before,

Layer by layer.

I now infect you,

Given my disease,

The intricate torture I pass one,

Shall bring you to your knees.

Releasing my vehemence upon you,

Do you like feeling all of this?

You left me with nothing,

Now you leave me bliss.

Now you see how it is,

This is the only way,

A glimpse into the hell,

That is my life everyday.

Hidden

Inside our heads exists a doorway,

A doorway to our private hell,

Here rests an eternal demon,

Using our misery as a place to dwell.

Others come,

Intentionally planting the seed,

The seed he uses,

He uses to make our minds bleed.

Lurking around, howling in the wind,

Hidden so deep inside,

Causing the insanity,

From which you cannot hide.

He lies within the depths,

My Monster Within

Bound and locked inside a cage,
He counts the seconds,
Waiting to unleash his rage.

Knocking and lingering through time,
Standing at the other side of the door,
The walls are shattering,
Can't hold him inside any more.

Shall he kill,
What will it be,
He releases his will,
Upon both you and me.

Now he walks alone,
Nobody is immune,
Slaughtering all in his way,
Kills platoon by platoon.

Now it's too late,
All is said and done,
Treating everybody in sight,
Like God's lost son.

Returning to which he came,

Leaving a trail of death,

Nobody will ever be the same,

There is nobody, nobody left.

Back inside his box,

It is time once again to sleep,

Restoring the energy,

For future lives to reap.

<u>Hate</u>

Is this me?

Why do I put on this mask?

Why do I look through these fake eyes?

Must I seem as you want me to?

Did you know me?

Did you know the scars you were leaving?

I hope there was a reason for building this abyss inside of
me.

Tired and attempted,

You made it all black,

My Monster Within

Time and energy has created me.

Do I scare you?

I feel it inside me,
Possesses and scratches at my soul,
So this is hell on earth.

Am I dreaming?

Now the demon lies inside me,
It cuts my internal self like a dorsal in the giant blue,
Peaking his head out when he feels necessary,
Changes me, the evil one has awoken.

Do I like this?

Do I want this?

Can I use this? ...... Yes I can.

This is me, the evil now boils deep inside,
I just do not care,

Why should I?,
None of you were fucking there,

Hate...I am...I love it...It is me...
Thank you.

<u>Alone</u>

[Just leave me alone,
  I don't want to hear your shit,
  I don't need anybody
  Only voice I hear,
  My own.]

Does my soul look very inviting?
You words act as a beast,
Smothering my spirit,
I can feel them biting,
Causing a visceral battle that I am,
Forced to be fighting.

Open your mouth,
keep pressing the buttons,
Oh what a grand fucking time,

My Monster Within

In my head this is where the fun ends.

[Just leave me alone,
  I don't want to hear your shit,
  I don't need anybody
  Only voice I hear,
  My own.]

Why should I bother?
Do I have to cater?
Pushing, pushing, pushing me so much farther,
Taking life, and making me turn to hate her.

Keep it up, oh what a shame,
I'm not going to be responsible,
I'm not going to be the one to blame,
Just leave me alone,
Keep it up, mother I feel like I'm going insane.

[Just leave me alone,
  I don't want to hear your shit,
  I don't need anybody
  Only voice I hear,

My own.]

My all is one,

In my scrutiny the rest are none,

Continue your activity,

Keep torturing me,

Forcing me to show you no pity

Is it that I act cryptic?

The hell you cause me,

I'll make sure that you also feel it

You insist on continuing,

I just want to be left alone.

Welcome to Society

Brought into this hectic world,

Born a baby with a clean slate.

Innocent mind soon to be changed,

This is it, what you must imitate.

Welcome to our world,

Life is full of eternal needs.

Enter the first light,

My Monster Within

The machine plants its seeds.

[Welcome to Society,
  Welcome to Society.]

Slanted with speech,
In there eyes I am alive.
Sculpt my figure,
It is the only way to survive.

Pressures from all angles, what should I do?
Desire to fit in, that is my only want.
Try and conform, I must be like you,
If I do not, they will all come to haunt.

[Welcome to Society,
  Welcome to Society.]

Shaped by pictures in a magazine,
And celebrities on tv.
Struggling to remain one
Burning it all to me.

My Monster Within

You all must open your eyes,

Open them and see,

This is how to act; this is how to breathe,

Because we say so, this is the way to be.

[Welcome to Society,

  Welcome to Society.]

Thoughts into my soul,

Burn.

Images carved in stone,

I yearn.

No outcast, no obesity,

To them there is no moral decency.

Oh the pain,

The pain,

Changing it all,

Every belief that I hold in my brain,

It hurts too much,

Not worth attempting to restrain.

My Monster Within

I must belong,

I must be apart,

Oh my individuality,

So fucking far gone.